Advance praise for

The Blueprint

How the Democrats Won Colorado
(and Why Republicans Everywhere Should Care)

"Every conservative should read *The Blueprint*. It is a must-read for anyone who wants to understand how the Left has built its machine."

—Redstate.com

"Colorado Democrats managed what most considered the impossible in the last decade…In *The Blueprint*, the strategy behind that success is detailed in a most engaging fashion."

—PoliticsDaily.com

"This book does a great job dissecting one of the most significant shifts in Colorado's political history. Adam Schrager and Rob Witwer chronicle not just the recent transformation of Colorado's political landscape, but they tell the fascinating story—from an insider's vantage point—of the people, personalities, and varied interests that were at the heart of it. It's a tale replete with valuable lessons the rest of the nation would be wise to heed."

—Colorado governor Bill Ritter (D)

"You may not know the names Pat Stryker and Tim Gill, but you should. They are the deep-pocket Democrats who led the Left's takeover of the center-right Rocky Mountain state. They and their team developed, funded, and executed a political strategy that undid a decade of Republican domination of Colorado politics and which is now being franchised across the country. That's the bad news. The good news is that Rob Witwer and Adam Schrager's book is all the intelligence every conservative needs on how to match and defeat such plans. They have reverse engineered the blueprint so everyone can learn the tactics and the strategy of the blueprint. If you care about the country and are involved at any level with politics, and especially if you are alarmed at the leftward lurch of the early Obama era, you need to read *The Blueprint*."

—Hugh Hewitt,
host of radio's nationally syndicated
The Hugh Hewitt Show

"[*The Blueprint*] is the first and only comprehensive book on how the Colorado political climate has turned from right-wing red to a progressive shade of blue. A must-read for every American who wishes to understand the art of building power at the state and local levels."

—Michael Huttner,
founder and CEO of ProgressNow

"If you want to know what's really happening at the cutting edge of campaigns and elections, read this book. *The Blueprint* is more than just an entertaining look behind the scenes of one of the most effective machines in American political history. It's a wake-up call for national Republicans to study, learn, and react to the lessons of Colorado."

—Bill Owens,
former governor of Colorado (R)

"In the last few years, Colorado Democrats learned the oldest lesson in the political playbook: that when you combine voter backlash with field organizing and a huge amount of cash, you can win elections. In *The Blueprint*, Adam Schrager and Rob Witwer have meticulously documented the ensuing tension between the genuinely exciting possibilities of grassroots progressive politics—and the simultaneously depressing problems that result when a handful of rich donors use millions of dollars to commandeer a political party."

—David Sirota,
nationally syndicated columnist,
author, and radio host

"Our lives and communities are shaped by political choices, and this fascinating book shows how a hidden world of interest groups, wealthy individuals, and activists shape these choices. Although campaign finance laws were supposed to clean up politics, *The Blueprint* shows how they have had just the opposite effect. If you care about the direction our country is taking, this book is essential reading."

—M. Todd Henderson,
professor of law,
University of Chicago Law School

"[On] Election night of 2004, Republicans in Colorado saw a light at the end of the tunnel. Unfortunately, it was a train. No one heard it coming or even knew it. It was called the Colorado Democracy Alliance. The engineer, a guy by the name of Tim Gill. So Republicans throughout the country, beware: build a better train or get run over by this one—it is headed your way."

—Tom Tancredo,
former US representative (R-CO)

"Adam Schrager and Rob Witwer have written an engaging and important book. It will be in high demand by folks ranging from political junkies and strategists to students and anyone interested in a great combination of political insight and entertainment. Readers will learn about the power of money—how the 'big four' (Tim Gill, Jared Polis, Rutt Bridges, and Pat Stryker) and others helped bankroll multiple groups and campaigns which then worked in coordinated fashion with one purpose in mind—namely, to produce Democratic winners. They'll see what the combination of good political instinct, smart organization, and technology can do. And they'll read about hapless Republicans who, after decades of enjoying the throne, were outspent, outfoxed, and left to wonder why so many voters no longer loved them."

—John Straayer,
professor of political science,
Colorado State University

"Adam Schrager and Rob Witwer have done some serious legwork and uncovered evidence of a startling transformation in American politics. They show how a small group of wealthy liberal activists in Colorado has essentially replaced the traditional Democratic Party organization with a new one that can work around campaign finance laws. What's more, they suggest that this new form of political party may be more efficient than the old one, as it's decentralized and more strategic in allocating campaign resources. The book shows how this new form of organization has transformed Colorado politics and affected state legislative races across the country in just a few short years."

—Seth Masket,
professor of political science,
University of Denver

The Blueprint

How the Democrats Won Colorado

(and Why Republicans
EVERYWHERE
Should Care)

Adam Schrager and Rob Witwer

Golden, Colorado

Library of Congress Control Number: 2010923205

Printed on SFI-certified paper in the United States of America by Malloy, Inc.

0 9 8 7 6 5 4 3

Design by Jack Lenzo
Cover: Dome image courtesy of Colorado State Archives

Speaker's Corner Books
An imprint of Fulcrum Publishing, Inc.
4690 Table Mountain Drive, Suite 100
Golden, Colorado 80403
800-992-2908 • 303-277-1623
www.speakerscornerbooks.com

Dramatis Personae

(On the Left)

Steve Adams—Former president of the Colorado American Federation of Labor—Congress of Industrial Organizations. Original member of the Roundtable

AFL-CIO—American Federation of Labor—Congress of Industrial Organizations

Matt Angle—Director of the Texas Democratic Trust

Bob Bacon—Current Colorado state senator (D)

Jennifer Brandeberry—Former government affairs director of the Colorado Trial Lawyers Association. Original member of the Roundtable

Rutt Bridges—Software developer and multimillionaire. Member of the Gang of Four

CCV—Colorado Conservation Voters

CEA—Colorado Education Association

CoDA—Colorado Democracy Alliance. A group of donors and political operatives who joined forces to fund progressive organizations and elect Democrats in Colorado. Successor to the Roundtable

Colorado Ethics Watch—CREW's Colorado affiliate

Colorado Media Matters—A now defunct progressive media watchdog group

CREW—Center for Responsibility and Ethics in Washington. A national watchdog group

CTLA—Colorado Trial Lawyers Association

Democracy Alliance—A national group of wealthy progressive donors

Mike Feeley—Former Colorado Senate minority leader (D)

Gang of Four—Rutt Bridges, Tim Gill, Jared Polis, and Pat Stryker

Beth Ganz—Former executive director of the Colorado chapter of the National Abortion Rights Action League. Original member of the Roundtable

Tim Gill—Founder of Quark, Inc., and gay-rights advocate. Member of the Gang of Four

Ellen Golombek—Former field director for the Colorado AFL-CIO and outgoing national political and field director for Planned Parenthood. Original member of the Roundtable

Mark Grueskin—Prominent Democratic attorney in Colorado

Brandon Hall—Former Democratic political operative in Colorado. Currently campaign manager for US Senate majority leader Harry Reid (D-NV)

Jill Hanauer—Democratic strategist. Original member of the Roundtable

Michael Huttner—Activist and founder of ProgressNow. Original member of the Roundtable

Paul Lhevine—Democratic strategist. Original member of the Roundtable

Alice Madden—Former Colorado state House majority leader. Original member of the Roundtable

Lynne Mason—Government affairs director of the Colorado Education Association. Original member of the Roundtable

Tony Massaro—Former executive director of Colorado Conservation Voters and current senior vice president for political affairs and public education for the League of Conservation Voters in Washington, DC. Original member of the Roundtable

Bill Menezes—Former director of Colorado Media Matters

NARAL—National Abortion Rights Action League

Ed Perlmutter—Former Colorado state senator and current US representative (D)

Jared Polis—Dot-com multimillionaire and current US representative (D-CO). Member of the Gang of Four

ProgressNow—Progressive grassroots organization

Bill Ritter—Current Colorado governor (D)

Roundtable—Group of donors, elected officials, strategists, and organizations that united to help Democrats win both chambers of the Colorado General Assembly in 2004. Predecessor to the Colorado Democracy Alliance

Ken Salazar—Former US senator (D-CO) and current US secretary of the interior

Rob Stein—Founder of Democracy Alliance

Pat Stryker—Billionaire. Member of the Gang of Four

Texas Democratic Trust—Progressive donor alliance that targets Texas state races

Ted Trimpa—Democratic strategist, advisor to Tim Gill, and key architect of the Democratic takeover in Colorado. Original member of the Roundtable

Mark Udall—Former US representative and current US senator (D-CO)

Al Yates—Democratic strategist, advisor to Pat Stryker, and key architect of the Democratic takeover in Colorado. Original member of the Roundtable

Laurie Hirschfeld Zeller—Former executive director of the Colorado Democracy Alliance

(On the Right)

Norma Anderson—Former Colorado Senate majority leader (R)

John Andrews—Former Colorado Senate president (R)

Julaine Appling—President of Wisconsin Family Action

Fred Barnes—National journalist, executive editor of *The Weekly Standard*, and contributor to Fox News. Barnes coined the phrase *Colorado Model* to describe the work of the Roundtable and CoDA from 2004 to 2008.

Bob Beauprez—Former US representative (R-CO) and unsuccessful candidate for Colorado governor in 2006

Bob Briggs—Former Colorado state representative (R)

Jon Caldara—President of the Independence Institute

Capital Research Center—A conservative Washington, DC, think tank

Danny Carroll—Former speaker pro tempore of the Iowa House of Representatives (R)

Sean Duffy—Republican strategist and former deputy chief of staff to Colorado governor Bill Owens

Rob Fairbank—Former Colorado state representative (R)

Pam Groeger—Former Colorado state representative (R)

Ted Harvey—Former Colorado state representative and current Colorado state senator (R)

J. A. "Doc" Hines—Former Wisconsin state representative (R)

Independence Institute—A conservative/libertarian Colorado-based think tank

Ramey Johnson—Former Colorado state representative (R)

Brad Jones—Founder of the conservative news organization Face the State

Keith King—Former Colorado House of Representatives majority leader and current Colorado state senator (R)

Matt Knoedler—Former Colorado state representative and unsuccessful candidate for Colorado Senate in 2006 (R)

Doug Lamborn—Former Colorado state senator and current US representative (R)

Ray Martinez—Former mayor of Fort Collins, Colorado, and unsuccessful candidate for Colorado Senate in 2004 (R)

Marilyn Musgrave—Former US representative (R-CO)

Bill Owens—Former Colorado governor (R)

Alan Philp—Former executive director of the Colorado Republican Party, former executive director of the Trailhead Group, and current regional political director for the Republican National Committee

Ellen Roberts—Current Colorado state representative (R)

Bob Schaffer—Former US representative (R-CO) and unsuccessful candidate for US Senate in 2008

Lola Spradley—Former Speaker of the Colorado House of Representatives (R)

Trailhead Group—527 organization founded by conservative donors, elected officials, and political strategists to help elect conservative candidates in 2006

Matthew Vadum—Researcher and writer at the Capital Research Center

Vitale & Associates—A Colorado-based Republican political consulting firm

Contents

Preface

For the better part of the past decade, we watched this story unfold from our front-row seats as a political reporter and a member of the Colorado House of Representatives. Yet neither of us truly grasped the significance of what was happening until it was over.

What started in a smoke-free conference room in Denver during the summer of 2004 has become a blueprint that is now being used by progressives to win political races across the country. And as this book explains, there is also a direct link between the Rockies and the White House.

When we sat down to discuss this project, we gave ourselves a challenge: share a political story without writing a "political book." Political people will draw their own conclusions, but the basic facts of the story should be of great interest to all. We also found that this story involves some intriguing human drama, and we hope to show the motivations and actions of the players as fully and fairly as possible.

We interviewed dozens of people and read hundreds of public documents, including media reports, campaign finance filings, and Internal Revenue Service disclosures. These were supplemented with internal memoranda and data provided by sources from both sides of the aisle. Sources, for the most part, are quoted by name or by publication. We have sought to be as transparent as possible, realizing the inherent mistrust the general public has for both journalists and elected officials.

Along the route, our biggest criticism from some has been that we refrain from passing judgment on the information we discovered. We hope that is the case, as the facts will no doubt elicit a variety of responses from readers without our interference.

As with all projects of this magnitude, it is impossible to give enough thanks to everyone who gave their time and their thoughts. However, we'd be remiss if we did not mention the following people by name (listed in alphabetical order).

Current and former governors: Dick Lamm, Bill Owens, and Bill Ritter

Current and former members of Congress: Bob Beauprez, Ed Perlmutter, Jared Polis, and Tom Tancredo

Donors and advisors: Tim Gill, Ted Trimpa, Al Yates, and Michael Huttner

Current and former state representatives: Norma Anderson, Bob Briggs, Danny Carroll (Iowa), Rob Fairbank, Gwyn Green, Ramey Johnson, Matt Knoedler, Alice Madden, Bob McCluskey, Amy Stephens, and Paul Weissmann

Current and former state senators: John Andrews, Michael Feeley, Ted Harvey, Evie Hudak, Keith King, Josh Penry, and Jeff Wells

Former candidates: Affie Ellis and Libby Szabo

Political consultants, lobbyists, journalists, and other professionals: J. J. Ament, Charles Ashby, Katy Atkinson, Randy Bangert, Anne Barkis, Fred Barnes, Lynn Bartels, Mike Beasley, Doug Bell, Vincent Carroll, Scott Chase, Floyd Ciruli, Evan Dreyer, Jonathan

Ellis, Sandra Fish, Beth Ganz, Scott Gessler, Ben Ginsberg, Ellen Golombek, Dan Haley, Jill Hanauer, Hugh Hewitt, Brad Jones, Stephen Keating, Greg Kolomitz, Dan Kully, Paul Lhevine, Rich Lowry, Lynne Mason, Tony Massaro, Bill McGinley, John J. Miller, Wendy Norris, Ramesh Ponnuru, Mike Potemra, Mike Saccone, Shelly Schafer, Geitner Simmons, David Sirota, Jason Steorts, Danny Tomlinson, Todd Vitale, Steve Welchert, and Terry Whitney

Academics, librarians, and nonelected public servants: Rich Coolidge (Colorado secretary of state's office), Joe Heim (University of Wisconsin—La Crosse), M. Todd Henderson (University of Chicago Law School), Robert Loevy (Colorado College), Seth Masket (University of Denver), Gay Roesch (Colorado Legislative Council), and John Straayer (Colorado State University)

Political party officers and staffers: Alan Philp, Katie Reinisch, Dick Wadhams, and Pat Waak

Think tank and nonprofit officers: Matt Angle, Julaine Appling, Jon Caldara, Jessica Corry, Ben Degrow, Ben Gregory (Colorado Conservation Voters), Mike McCabe (Wisconsin Democracy Campaign), Bill Menezes, Lynne Munson, Mario Sanchez, Isaac Smith, Rob Stein, and Matthew Vadum

We would like to thank the *National Review* and *The Omaha World-Herald* for understanding the early value of this story.

Numerous people including Matt Arnold, Adam Bonin, Dan Currell, Steven Duffield, Mark Feiner, Sara Gandy, Ray Gifford, Dan Hopkins, David London,

Leslie Oliver, Jeff Posternak, Lee Reichert, Lyle Roberts, and Jean Witwer helped shape the narrative throughout the process.

We would not be where we are with this manuscript if not for the intellectual curiosity of Sam Scinta and his team at Fulcrum Publishing, particularly Katie Wensuc, Carolyn Sobczak, and Jack Lenzo. Fulcrum's Speaker's Corner series has stimulated conversations throughout the country on topics ranging from healthcare to prosecutorial conduct. We hope the following story serves the same purpose.

Finally, we'd like to thank our wives, Heather and Cathy, and our children (John, Robby, Jeffrey, and Christopher Witwer, and Harper and Clark Schrager) for understanding why this story is important to tell. Our blueprint for true happiness rests with them.

Introduction

August 2008:
The Democratic National Convention—
How This Story Ends

For six days in August, it felt more like Cannes than Denver.

Not that the Starz Green Room is terribly glamorous—quite the contrary. The art-house theater is just one wing of a sprawling nineteenth-century red-brick building called the Tivoli Center, which serves as the student union for three local colleges. If you wanted action and prime-time TV audiences, the Pepsi Center across the street seemed a better bet.

But appearances can be deceptive. During the 2008 Democratic National Convention, the Green Room's VIP-only admittance policy and high-powered programs set it apart from other venues in town. In a city full of elite A-listers, the Green Room was the place to be seen. Here, movie stars, celebrity bloggers, Washington journalists, and elected officials could pass the time in relative privacy while awaiting the nightly parade of headliner speeches.

The Hollywood paparazzi and Washington media who gathered about the entrance were not disappointed. Their cameras captured some of the well-known faces who were in Denver that week: James Hoffa, Charlize Theron, John Podesta, Kal Penn (of *Harold & Kumar Go to White Castle* fame), Walter Isaacson, James Carville, several members of

Congress, and Will.i.am of the Black Eyed Peas.

Those lucky enough to get into the Green Room could relax in the lounge, catch an indie film, or attend panels on hot political topics.

In one program, blogger Arianna Huffington, Jonathan Alter of *Newsweek*, and Chris Cilizza of *The Washington Post* talked about the role of new media in modern politics. In another, Hollywood stars Josh Brolin, Ben Affleck, and Rosario Dawson gave readings from an upcoming film based on socialist author Howard Zinn's *A People's History of the United States*.

The air in the lounge buzzed with anticipation. National Democrats had gathered in Denver once before, exactly a century earlier. Back then, they picked Nebraska orator and three-time presidential candidate William Jennings Bryan to carry the party's banner into the general election. It ended in disaster, with Bryan losing the electoral college by a humiliating 321–162 margin.

This time was going to be different. Although the election was still nine weeks away, Democratic insiders confidently discussed what they didn't dare say in public: this thing was over. Barack Obama was going to be the next president, no doubt about it.

And the best part? His historic nomination would take place in the heart of the Rocky Mountain West, right under the noses of a Republican Party that had, until recently, dominated the region's politics.

No cameras were clicking as Rob Stein walked into Theater 8 of the Green Room just before ten o'clock that Wednesday morning. But to Democratic operatives, the well-dressed Albert Brooks look-alike was one of the biggest celebrities in Denver.

Stein was there to moderate a panel entitled "Democracy Alliance: Colorado as a Model—Donor Cooperation for Social Change." He, better than anyone, understood the secret electoral formula discovered by Colorado Democrats in the previous forty-eight months. Many believed that formula was a blueprint for future Democratic success across the nation.

The former Bill Clinton staffer was known for his famous PowerPoint presentation, called "The Conservative Message Machine Money Matrix," which detailed how the Right had built a thriving network of think tanks and independent organizations to help elect conservative candidates. One such institution, the Heritage Foundation, was founded with the financial support of Joe Coors, whose grandfather built a brewery in the town of Golden, just a few miles west of where Stein now walked.

For years, Stein carried his electronic slideshow around the country trying to beg, borrow, or steal a few minutes in front of Democratic Party leaders and wealthy progressive* donors.

The Left, Stein argued, needed its own infrastructure. Would they help him build it?

---

*The word *progressive* has, of late, replaced the word *liberal* as the most popular generic term meaning "left-leaning."

Stein's message slowly caught on in the early to mid-2000s with donors like financier George Soros, Hollywood director Rob Reiner, and Taco Bell heir Rob McKay. Enlisting the financial resources of more than eighty deep-pocketed benefactors, Stein founded the Democracy Alliance in 2005 to help build the progressive infrastructure that had until then existed only in his mind.

Meanwhile, and quite independently of Stein, a small group of Colorado progressives had put the substance of Stein's vision into practice with great success—one year *before* Democracy Alliance opened its doors. In 2004, several wealthy donors and a network of united progressive organizations helped make Colorado—until recently, a reliably Republican state—a deep shade of blue.

They called it the Colorado Miracle.

To the insiders in Theater 8, the Colorado Miracle needed no explanation. In October 2004, the GOP dominated politics at every level in Colorado. Republicans held both US Senate seats, five of seven congressional seats, the governor's mansion, the secretary of state's and treasurer's offices, and both houses of the state legislature. On Election Day in 2008, the opposite would be true.

By any measure, it was one of the most stunning reversals of fortune in American political history.

Even taking national trends into account, the success of Colorado Democrats was extraordinary. While changing demographics and an unpopular president played a part, they could not explain the complete and total domination the Left achieved in such a short time.

As national Republicans cruised to victory in 2004, winning the presidency and moving six US Senate seats into the GOP column, Colorado Democrats captured both houses of the state legislature, flipped a congressional seat, and provided one of only two Democratic pickups in the US Senate (the other being Obama in Illinois). From 2004 to 2008, Colorado Democrats consistently outperformed their peers in other states, even as Republicans held a statewide voter registration advantage.

The Colorado Miracle was one of the reasons the convention was held in Denver that year. And with Obama up in the polls, the state was in play for a Democratic presidential candidate for only the second time in four decades.

This was a story worth telling.

"Had we been here four years ago, on this exact same date," Stein began, "there would have been virtually no credible capabilities that we could talk about that in any way, shape, or form could be seen as fairly competitive with the enormous machinery that the Right has built."

"But," he continued, "there has never, in the history of progressivedom, been a clearer, more strategic, more focused, more disciplined, better financed group of institutions operating at the state and national level."

Stein then introduced Laurie Hirschfeld Zeller, executive director of the Colorado Democracy

Alliance (CoDA). Zeller's presentation was CoDA's public debut, and a proclamation of the organization's pivotal role in transforming Colorado.

"At CoDA, we're very proud to be the poster child for state-based collaboratives," she said. "We embrace the progressive label in our giving and in the strategic role that we play in Colorado politics. Our job is to build a long-term progressive infrastructure in Colorado while we're conceding nothing in the short term, in terms of progressive goals at the ballot box."

"I've been struck," she mused, "[that] as friends from out of town are coming here for the convention, [they] are pleased to find a sophisticated modern city here. I think they pictured a frontier town and we were encircling the wagons, surrounded by hostile red, conservative populations."

Carrying the metaphor forward and then mixing it a bit, she had a message for progressives: "The tents have been struck and we're building a community here. There's an irrigation system in place that is going to provide a harvest later this fall but that's also building a community and building an infrastructure for the long term."

Stein jumped in. "And in the absolutely finest form of flattery," he said, "*The Weekly Standard*, which is the most respected conservative-right opinion journal in the country, did a cover story about a month ago, written by Fred Barnes, on the Colorado Model."

"And it is a warning shot to conservatives in America that if the Colorado Model is replicated elsewhere, conservatives have nothing comparable to possibly compete with it, and they had better watch out."

The crowd erupted with applause. From the back, someone shouted, "Yea, Colorado!"

"'Yea, Colorado,' is exactly right!" Stein replied. "And it really is the model."

The message electrified the audience: Colorado was just the beginning. Only thirty-four hours later and less than a mile away, Obama would accept the Democratic nomination for president of the United States. But Stein had something bigger in mind. He wasn't just talking about winning the White House—he was talking about Democrats taking over political offices at every level of government from coast to coast for years to come.

"The reason it is so important to control government is because government is the source of enormous power," Stein continued. "One president in this country, when he or she takes office, appoints...5,000 people to run a bureaucracy, nonmilitary nonpostal service of 2 million people, who hire 10 million outside outsource contractors—a workforce of 12 million people—that spends $3 trillion a year. That number is larger than the gross domestic product of all but four countries on the face of the earth."

"So the reason we're doing what we're doing... and the way we get progressive change, is to control government," Stein said. "That's what this is about."

And that's where Colorado came in. Announcing "a quiet little project" called the Committee on States, Stein proposed, through the Democracy

Alliance, to duplicate the Colorado Miracle in eighteen other states over the next twenty months. "As we know, 2010 is redistricting, there are thirty-five governors' races, so it's going to be a critically important year," Stein said.

To prepare for 2010, architects of the Colorado Miracle would be working hard to get progressives in other states "up to Colorado's level of sophistication and organizational development," Stein went on.

As Stein knew, there was nothing terribly complicated about what Colorado progressives did. First, they built a robust network of nonprofit entities to replace the Colorado Democratic Party, which had been rendered obsolete by campaign-finance reform. Second, they raised historic amounts of money from large donors to fund these entities. Third, they recruited candidates with longstanding ties to their communities. Fourth, they developed a consistent, topical message about their strengths and the opposition's weaknesses. Fifth, and most important, they put aside their policy differences to focus on the common goal of winning elections.

As former Colorado Democratic House majority leader Alice Madden later said, "It's not rocket science."

Barnes was one of the first conservatives outside the state to take notice of what was going on in Colorado. The executive editor of *The Weekly Standard* warned that "[t]here's something unique going on in Colorado that, if copied in other states, has the potential to produce sweeping Democratic gains nationwide...With enough money, its main elements can no doubt be replicated in other states."

And money was precisely Stein's point. In the past thirty months, he told the crowd, Democracy Alliance donors had put more than $110 million into thirty state-level groups. As Stein put it, "There are a bunch of states where over the next couple of years a lot of development is going to happen."

Later in the presentation, some of those states were discussed: Maine, Michigan, Minnesota, New Mexico, North Carolina, Ohio, Utah, Wisconsin, and Wyoming.

For Republicans in those states and beyond, understanding what happened in Colorado is more than a matter of curiosity—it may be a matter of political survival.

For Democrats, this is a story of unprecedented success.

As audience members filed out of Theater 8 into the midday sun, it began to sink in that the Colorado Miracle was no mere one-off success.

Colorado was the blueprint.

Part One
The Gang of Four

Chapter One

Jared Polis:
Colorado's Political Past Meets the Future—
in Arizona

The sun had barely broken above the hills near Hi Corbett Field in Tucson, Arizona, and already they were out there stretching, throwing, and running. They wore black jerseys, white pants, and a silver-billed hat with the purple letters *CR*.

Colorado Rockies manager Clint Hurdle walked among them, joking and prodding about some missed assignment or broken play from the day before. Pitching coach Bob Apodaca talked mechanics with some of his pupils, using terms like "arm slot" and "quick feet."

There were dozens of men in the prime of their careers. Those careers just didn't happen to include baseball.

Rockies Fantasy Camp introduced CEOs, CPAs, and MDs to different acronyms, like RBIs and ERAs. But the session in February 2003, a week before spring training started, was unique.

Unlike years past, when men used to making headlines could learn the game from the experts without fear of publicity, this week would be chronicled by the Denver media. Reporters were there to follow the progress of the state's leading baseball fan and a former high school pitcher, Governor Bill Owens.

"I think he's been spending too much time in

the office," Hurdle joked of the state's chief executive after he whiffed on a number of pitches during batting practice. "I just think he's a little nervous. I told him nobody gets released from Fantasy Camp, nobody gets sent down. There's no Triple A governorship that he's going to have to go to if he doesn't do well here."

Owens was certainly doing well in a different type of hardball. Just a few months earlier, the second-term Republican governor had won reelection with more than 64 percent of the vote, and he presided over one of the strongest state Republican establishments in the country.

"We controlled everything but the courts," said Alan Philp, a former executive director for the Colorado Republican Party. With a voter registration advantage hovering between 150,000 and 200,000 and strong party organization, the GOP was in good shape for the foreseeable future. "Nobody seriously thought Colorado was anything but a Republican-leaning state," Philp recalled.

This view was borne out at the ballot box. Of the state's seven congressional districts, only two—the Denver and Boulder seats—were held by Democrats. Ben Nighthorse Campbell, who had switched to the Republican Party in 1995, was the state's senior US senator, where he served with Republican Wayne Allard, who in 2002 handily defeated Democrat Tom Strickland for the second time in six years. At the

2000 Republican National Convention in Philadelphia, the Colorado delegation enjoyed prime seating in the front row below the podium, reflecting the state's position as a bulwark in the Republican-friendly Rocky Mountain West.

In the state legislature, Republicans enjoyed a longstanding historical advantage, often controlling the state House and Senate by margins of two or more Republicans for every Democrat. In the past forty years, there were only three brief intervals when the GOP *didn't* control both chambers. The first was in 1964, when Democrats rode Lyndon B. Johnson's landslide victory over Barry Goldwater to capture the state House. That lasted two years. In 1976, Watergate gave House Democrats another window of control. That, too, lasted just two years.

The only other taste of success for legislative Democrats was in 2000, and in retrospect it proved a harbinger of things to come. Ironically, that victory—capturing the Senate from 2000 to 2002—was at least in part made possible by a former Republican state senator, Terry Considine. As part of the term-limits movement, Considine formed an organization called Coloradans Back in Charge to place term limits on the 1990 Colorado ballot.

Considine, who was profiled in publications like the *National Review,* was privately scorned by some of his legislative colleagues at home. But he thought two four-year terms for statewide officers and state senators and four two-year terms for state representatives should be more than enough time to

accomplish their policy goals. It would de-profession-
alize politics, Considine argued, giving meaning to
the term *citizen legislature.*

In November 1990, an overwhelming 71 percent of Colorado voters agreed. While the part of
the amendment that related to members of Congress
was later struck down by the US Supreme Court, the
first wave of term-limited—and mostly Republican—
state representatives and senators was set to leave
office before the end of the decade.

Demographics brought 1 million people to Colorado in the 1990s—transplants from places like
California, Texas, and the Midwest—who tended to
be less rigid in their political affiliation. So while
Republicans saw a policy victory in the success of
term limits, Democrats saw that a window of opportunity would open in 1998, the year the new law officially kicked in.

The net effect of term limits was to create contested seats in districts that had previously been
held by long-established Republican incumbents.
Emboldened, Democratic leaders hatched a plan to
retake the state Senate for the first time since John
F. Kennedy was president.

"We had an all-out push in 2000," recalled Mike
Feeley, the Senate minority leader. "We raised more
money and took a more systematic approach. We
were very selective about recruiting candidates."

Feeley's $1.5 million coordinated campaign was
like nothing Democrats in Colorado had ever done
before. There was a campaign manager in every

targeted district. Messaging was tested and calibrated according to polling data. For once, Democrats weren't throwing darts at a board.

With the Colorado Education Association (CEA), Colorado's largest teacher's union, and the Colorado American Federation of Labor—Congress of Industrial Organizations (AFL-CIO) coordinating resources with the state party to focus on a few races in the western suburbs of Denver, Democrats entered Election Day with a hope they hadn't entertained before. One reporter called their last-minute get-out-the-vote efforts the "poster campaign for carpal tunnel syndrome" because of the phone banks they had set up.

Democrats focused their energy on the traditionally Republican stronghold of Jefferson County, in the suburbs west of Denver. There, three women in particular—Sue Windels, Joan Fitz-Gerald, and Deanna Hanna—seemed poised to take over historically GOP-leaning Senate seats. Other Democrats chafed at the lack of support they would receive during the 2000 cycle, but Feeley and his coalition had determined that this year it would all come down to those three women.

"People were very hesitant about funding because they didn't believe we could do it," said Ellen Golombek, who ran the field efforts for Colorado's AFL-CIO in 2000 and who is the outgoing national political and field director for Planned Parenthood. "We had to beg and scrape for the resources."

Hanna's race was called in her favor shortly after 10:00 PM, lifting spirits at the Election Day party at

Denver's historic Oxford Hotel. "It's an emotional roller coaster," Feeley told reporters. "We're still waiting to confirm, but it looks really good. It looks really good."

Shortly before midnight, the Democrats got the news they were waiting for.

"Fitz-Gerald and Windels both just came in...It's all over!" Feeley screamed to the crowd. "We're at eighteen! We won the majority!"

One of his Senate colleagues (and current US representative), Ed Perlmutter, grabbed a news photographer by the shoulders and mugged for the camera. "We're going to Disneyland!" he shouted.

To everyone involved in later Democratic successes, what happened in 2000 was essential.

"The Colorado Miracle was actually 2000," Golombek said. "One of the Republicans said something like, 'They played dirtier than we did. I didn't think they had it in them.' We didn't play dirty. We played honest—just brought out more facts than ever before."

Feeley, himself a casualty of term limits, concluded his eight years in the state Senate on a high note. "I went down swinging," he said with a laugh.

For Governor Owens, losing the Senate was a setback—and not one he was willing to accept, either. For the next two years, he worked with GOP leaders to ensure that the anomalous Democratic victory remained just that—an anomaly. With a ferocious effort, Republicans managed to recapture the Senate in 2002, albeit by a tenuous 18–17 margin.

Having beaten back the Democrats, Governor Owens was firmly in control of the Capitol. After his reelection, he was named "America's Best Governor" by the *National Review*. Republicans around the country noticed his success in cutting taxes, pushing for the country's first-ever simultaneous mass transit/highway expansion project, and an innovative education reform program that stressed accountability. He was even being discussed in some circles as a future presidential contender.

But if you asked him what his dream job was, it would have been to be at spring training for real, first as a player and then as a coach, manager, or even team owner.

At Fantasy Camp, Owens wore number seventeen in honor of Rockies first baseman Todd Helton, one of the team's best players and the one who could be found in the spotlight ever since being drafted in the first round by the franchise.

Like Helton would be the following week when spring training officially opened, Owens was mobbed. Everyone wanted to shake his hand, to play on his team, to offer a compliment.

"Wild Bill," Hurdle shouted while Owens worked on his pitching, "bringing the pain!" Owens wasn't a bad hitter either, posting a hefty .400 average for the week.

For the governor's part, he simply wanted to blend in, asking his fellow campers to call him Bill.

"Down here, I'm just Bill." But from the sales executive who worried about "throwing inside" when the governor was batting to the umpires hired to work the games who knew "to give him the outside corner" when he was pitching, he might as well have been wearing a different-colored jersey.

The one person not in awe wore number four and was an avid Rockies fan himself, with prime season tickets right behind home plate. Twenty-seven-year-old Jared Polis was the vice chairman of the Colorado State Board of Education and an emerging factor in Colorado Democratic politics.

Growing up in San Diego, Polis fell in love with politics at a young age. When a developer tried to build homes where he and his brother played, Polis led the charge against the proposal at a city council meeting. He was eleven.

At sixteen, he headed off to Princeton, where he majored in political science and cofounded American Information Systems, an Internet service provider. While many of his classmates were drinking beer and getting ready to head off to Wall Street or law school, Polis spent his senior year on the road, drumming up financing for the company he would later sell for $20 million.

In the 1960s, Polis's parents formed a company called Blue Mountain Arts that sold poetry books and greeting cards. Recognizing the opportunities in the nascent dot-com space, Polis helped them create an online presence for the company, called BlueMountain.com. Although it wasn't profitable, three years later Excite@Home offered the family $700 million for it. Polis's personal take was an estimated $150 million, which he parlayed into another successful business venture, this one called ProFlowers. In 2005, Liberty Media Corporation bought ProFlowers and its parent company for $477 million.

Polis had joined Michael Dell, Tiger Woods, Jennifer Lopez, and Jeff Gordon on *Fortune*'s list of "rich kids." With an estimated $174 million to his name, Polis had more money than Britney Spears at the peak of her popularity.

Still in his twenties, Polis now had a nest egg that would allow him to pursue his real passion— politics—for the rest of his life. In 2000, he ran for the State Board of Education, a part-time, unpaid panel that oversees the Colorado Department of Education.

State board races are traditionally sleepy, low-profile affairs, but Polis approached the campaign as he would a business, investing heavily in his product, in this case himself. He plowed an unheard-of $1 million into his campaign.

Polis's Republican opponent, former state senator Ben Alexander, spent about $10,000. "At one point," Alexander told Robert Frank, author of *Richistan: A Journey through the American Wealth Boom and the Lives of the New Rich*, "when I heard he was willing to spend $1 million, I thought of writing him a letter saying, 'Let's split it in half. You give me $500,000 and I promise I'll drop out.'"

Polis beat Alexander by ninety votes out of nearly 1.6 million cast.

On the state board, Polis didn't shy away from controversy. To the dismay of some in the educational establishment, he advocated for charter schools and even founded his own chain of charters called the New America Schools, which served non-English-speaking immigrants.

And Polis was never afraid to play the young hipster card, as he did in 2002 when he submitted an editorial to the *Rocky Mountain News* entitled "Eminem: Why I Cotton to Mathers."

In it, Polis argued that the controversial white rapper Eminem (née Marshall Mathers) was "one of the preeminent vocal artists of the day." Far from being antisocial, Polis said, Eminem should be held up as a paragon of virtue. "While Mathers's art is inspired by being your bogeyman, he is actually one of the most relevant forces today promoting fidelity, safe sex, and traditional family values to a generation typically chastised as apathetic and anchorless," he continued.

"In a time when our elected leaders can't seem to discuss these matters in a way that is at all relevant to young people," Polis went on, "Mathers's message, including the missive 'now I'm frustrated cause my d--- was unprotected...' fills the void and speaks to teenagers in their own language."

Polis summed up his views by contrasting the frankness of Eminem's lyrics with what he considered the emptiness of contemporary political rhetoric. "We are lucky as a society to have someone of his talent and insight reaching such a mass audience with moral messages to fill a void that our so-called 'real' leaders refuse to address in a meaningful way. And, most important, his music rocks!"

In retrospect, Polis's public defense of Eminem was remarkable for a reason that wasn't obvious at the time. Even as Polis defended the rapper, gay and lesbian groups targeted Eminem's lyrics for promoting hatred against gays. Yet unbeknownst to Polis's readers or the general public whom he served in elected office, Polis himself was gay.

Four years later, he came out publicly in Boulder's *Daily Camera*, announcing that he had had a partner for the past two and a half years. "I think sexual orientation, like religion or race, has nothing to do with one's values, and to most people it's not important one way or the other," he told the paper.

It certainly wasn't important that day during Fantasy Camp, where Polis was focused on baseball, not politics. And truth be told, Polis is a pretty darn good ballplayer. "I'm telling you, he's got some skills," Rockies skipper Hurdle said. "He's a sleeper."

Polis and Owens met briefly in line waiting to shag fly balls where Rockies employee Chris "Snake" Rasnake was operating the ball machine providing the practice. The Owens-Polis handshake was more out of political necessity than genuine rapprochement, a meeting between the most successful politician in Colorado and the one who aspired to be.

Owens jogged to the outfield, camped out under a lazy fly ball, and confidently squeezed it into his mitt with two hands to the compliments of the coaches and those watching.

Polis was up next. He pulled down his sports goggles and sprinted out to the same green spot Owens had just occupied. He punched his hand into his glove and gave a thumbs-up that he was ready.

Rasnake tweaked the machine, smiled, and promptly sent a screaming line drive into the outfield that sent Polis running as the ball sailed over his head.

"That was a favor for [you]," Rasnake said to the governor as Polis scrambled to get the ball back into the infield.

"[You're] a good Republican, Snake," Owens called out. "All's fair in politics and baseball!"

The Boulder Democrat was also smiling when he returned to the line. The next time his turn came up, he pulled down the sports goggles and sprinted out to the spot in the outfield where the line drive had gone, punched his glove, and gave another thumbs-up.

When Snake tried to get him again by sending into the air the lazy fly ball he had given everybody else, Polis had to race in to catch it. But he caught it in full stride, earning admiration from the coaches.

"Nice adjustment, Polis," Hurdle said, and then he turned to Owens and the others. "He's a good player."

It wouldn't be the last time Jared Polis got the best of Colorado Republicans.

Chapter Two

Pat Stryker:
A Billionaire Decides to Spend Some Money

Al Yates was angry. "This has got to come to an end," he said as he left the Colorado Senate chamber. Walking through the glass doors, he spotted a friend in the crowded Senate lobby. "This is bullshit," Yates told him.

The outgoing Colorado State University (CSU) president had just been honored by senators with an official resolution celebrating his thirteen years at the helm of the Fort Collins institution. Dr. Yates, the first African American to hold the post, had by all accounts done an excellent job. But instead of being pleased, he was furious.

Earlier, as he sat on the red leather bench on the east side of the chamber, Yates bore witness to the extraordinary bitterness between the Senate's eighteen Republicans and seventeen Democrats. Just two days earlier, the Senate had erupted in a rancorous partisan battle over a bill to redraw the state's seven congressional districts, and today there were more contentious party-line votes on bills amending the state's campaign finance laws and requiring a daily recitation of the Pledge of Allegiance in public schools. Any semblance of legislative decorum was in shambles.

Yates waited. And waited. And grew more frustrated. And by the time the senators unanimously commended him for his "visionary, thoughtful, consistent, and often courageous leadership in the face of great challenges," something inside him snapped.

Two days earlier, Senate secretary Mona Heustis had stopped at a Kinko's near the Capitol before showing up for the start of the final week of the legislative session. What she brought to work that day infuriated Democratic lawmakers.

After the morning invocation, Senate Bill 352, a plan to redraw the borders of Colorado's seven congressional districts, was read into the record. Rumors had been rampant for the past four months about such a bill, and now it was here.

The congressional redistricting issue had been festering for more than three years. From 2000 to 2002, Democrats had enjoyed a brief and rare season of control over the Colorado Senate. Although it was just their second time in charge of a legislative chamber since 1976, their timing was impeccable—it happened to coincide with the constitutional requirement that states redraw congressional districts based on the 2000 census. Under the Colorado Constitution, the map would proceed through the legislative process as would any other bill, passing both chambers before being signed into law by the governor.

But Senate Democrats and House Republicans were at loggerheads on redistricting, and no compromise was forthcoming. Former state senator John

Andrews (who would later serve as Senate president) recalled one hearing in which the Democratic committee chairman asked a Republican map sponsor if he would like a cigarette and blindfold before his bill was killed. In Andrews's view, Senate Democrats had no interest in passing a redistricting bill through the process established by the state constitution. "They ran out the clock," he said. "It was their intention all along to force it into the courts, where they liked their chances."

After the end of the 2001 legislative session, Democrats filed a lawsuit in Denver District Court to settle the stalemate. At the end of the litigation, Judge John Coughlin, who had been appointed by Democratic governor Richard Lamm, selected a Democratic map from the host of proposals offered by the two political parties and several other groups.

On the basis of voter performance numbers, Coughlin's map created three Republican-leaning districts, two Democratic-leaning districts, and two competitive districts. For Democrats, whose share of Colorado's registered voters (30 percent) trailed both Republicans (36 percent) and unaffiliated voters (34 percent), the Coughlin map represented a significant victory, giving them a realistic chance of winning four of the state's seven congressional seats. Disappointed Republicans appealed Coughlin's decision but lost in the state supreme court. The redistricting battle, it seemed, was over.

Or so everyone thought.

In November 2002, Republicans recaptured the

Colorado Senate, and with victory came a new conversation among GOP senators: the state constitution said that the legislature, not a court, was supposed to draw congressional districts. With divided government, that didn't happen. But now the governor's office and both chambers were in the hands of a single party, so why shouldn't the legislature fulfill its constitutional obligation and draw a new map?

Early in the legislative session, Senate president John Andrews raised the possibility with Senator Norma Anderson, the Republican majority leader. The relationship between Andrews and Anderson, which was chilly to begin with, wasn't improved by the conversation. "This isn't going to help us any," Anderson told Andrews. Citing state budget problems as a reason to delay, she thought the GOP should wait awhile before doing something that might generate so much controversy.

What Anderson didn't know at that time, but soon found out, was that Colorado's redistricting map was on the minds of some very powerful people in Washington. Late in the legislative session, she received a call from the 202 area code with a name she didn't recognize. Anderson, assuming it was a reporter, was busy and didn't return it.

Several days later, Andrews popped his head into her office and asked, "Why didn't you return Karl Rove's call?"

"Who's Karl Rove?" Anderson replied.

Andrews explained that Rove was President George W. Bush's top political advisor. Anderson, who had always been more focused on state politics than national, called Rove back on his direct line.

Rove was just checking in to make sure the redistricting effort was moving along.

On the Thursday before the bill was ultimately introduced, Anderson expressed her concern to a few of her Senate colleagues. "You guys should not do this," she said. "This bill should not be introduced." She had a gut feeling it was a bad idea. She didn't like the politics, and although she wasn't a lawyer, she didn't think it was likely to hold up in court.

"They all turned and looked at me as if I was crazy," Anderson recalled. But Andrews had already counted votes in the Republican caucus, and Anderson was outvoted. So she capitulated. "I was majority leader," she said later. "I have to support my caucus."

And so with the introduction of Senate Bill 352, the redistricting battle was reopened. The new Republican map kept the essential features of Judge Coughlin's with two key differences: it changed the highly competitive seventh district to a Republican-leaning seat and it made the competitive third congressional district a safe Republican seat.

Democrats were apoplectic. Senators screamed at one another. There were accusations of intimidation. Allegations of lawlessness. Democrats tried to filibuster, in part asking first that the bill be read at length. Republicans were prepared, bringing in numerous staffers, more than a dozen in all, to read pages simultaneously to meet the legal requirement.

At the microphone, Senate minority leader Joan Fitz-Gerald called it a "kangaroo proceeding," a "travesty," and a "charade."

Republicans countered, saying it was the legislature's constitutional duty to redistrict the congressional lines after each census, not a judge's. "The public and the legislature are getting a lot more give-and-take on this bill than when an unelected judge made the decision by himself," said the bill's sponsor, Senator Doug Lamborn, a Republican from Colorado Springs. "The constitution tells us we have to do this. That is why we're here today."

Through it all, assistant minority leader Ken Gordon, a Democrat from Denver, kept shaking his head in disbelief. He predicted it wouldn't happen because, he said of his Republican colleagues, "They're not *all* dumb."

Just before midnight, Fitz-Gerald led her sixteen Democratic colleagues out of the chambers and the reredistricting bill passed on an 18–0 vote.

One clerk cried. Two staffers would later resign in protest. As the bill worked its way to the governor's desk to become law, the editorial board of *The Denver Post* weighed in, labeling Senate Bill 352 the "Midnight Gerrymander," a term it would repeat often. The press coverage was almost universally negative for Republicans.

Although the Colorado Supreme Court would later overturn Senate Bill 352, by then, for some political watchers in Colorado it had acquired indelible symbolic meaning of what was wrong with the

Republican Party. Democratic leaders nurtured that sentiment, recognizing that their greatest defeat might also prove to be an opportunity to unite against a common enemy. "It became a rallying point for Democrats and was used to point out the meanness of the Republican leadership," later said former Democratic state senator Mike Feeley.

Senate Bill 352 was also a rallying point for Yates. Speaking of it later, he said, "I was appalled, and it was at that moment I realized the future of our state was in jeopardy, and worse, our democracy was at risk." The redistricting episode "was strong evidence that keeping and expanding power was far more important to those in power than addressing the needs of our state and its citizens."

Truth be told, Yates was unhappy with Republicans in the state legislature long before that. In 2002, the state suffered revenue shortfalls as a result of the post-9/11 economic downturn. Budget cuts hit higher education hard, and Yates had been one of those who had unsuccessfully lobbied lawmakers to provide more funding.

After his visit to the Senate chamber, Yates picked up the phone and called his friend Pat Stryker. During Yates's tenure at CSU, he had come to know the divorced mother of three and fellow Fort Collins resident well. In 2005, a Denver magazine described Stryker as one who "could slip unobserved into a

PTA meeting or join a group of soccer moms and never seem out of place."

Unlike most PTA members and soccer moms, however, Stryker, worth nearly $1 billion, appeared on the *Forbes* 400 list of the richest people in America.

Stryker's fortune came primarily from her inherited interest in the Stryker Corporation, which describes itself as "a broadly based global leader in medical technology." Founded in 1941 by her grandfather, Dr. Homer Stryker, the company first innovated mobile hospital beds and has since grown into a publicly traded Fortune 500 corporation with 15,000 employees. Stryker is currently the fifth largest shareholder in the company, owning nearly 25 million shares of its common stock.

Stryker was no stranger to spending big money on political efforts. Two years earlier, a group called English for the Children had placed an initiative on the Colorado ballot that would have required all public school classes (other than foreign language classes) to be taught in English. It was known as Amendment 31. Stryker would soon become the measure's most effective opponent.

English for the Children was part of a greater effort by California technology entrepreneur Ron Unz, who in the late 1990s and early 2000s bankrolled a number of ballot initiatives in several states designed to roll back bilingual education and replace it with statewide English immersion policies. Unz's idea typically did well at the ballot box. In 1998, California voters approved it with 61 percent of the vote, and Arizona and Massachusetts voters, in 2000 and 2002 respectively, approved similar proposals with even greater margins.

When the *Rocky Mountain News* ran a poll testing public sentiment in early 2002, Colorado voters favored Amendment 31 by a margin of 68–24. At the time, Stryker's daughter attended Harris Bilingual Immersion School in Fort Collins, where she was learning English and Spanish in a dual-language program. "Mom," Stryker's daughter told her, "they're trying to close my school."

"When I learned who 'they' were and what they intended with this ballot issue," Stryker told the *Rocky Mountain News*, "I became active, along with other parents, in working to defeat it." Explaining her rationale, Stryker said, "For me, the issues are simple: Amendment 31 takes educational freedom of choice away from parents. It threatens teachers. It's bad for education and bad for the children of Colorado."

That July, Denver political consultant John Britz drove to Fort Collins to meet with Stryker about a possible donation to English Plus, a group formed to fight the measure. According to the *Rocky Mountain News*, Stryker asked Britz if he could guarantee victory for $3 million. Britz said he couldn't make any guarantees, but with that much money he could "break the code" and find a way to defeat Amendment 31.

Britz drove back to Denver with a $3 million commitment.

English Plus kept Stryker's contribution quiet until the last few weeks of the campaign. "We decided to wait until October 1," Britz's partner Steve Welchert told the *Rocky Mountain News*, "and played poor, poor, pitiful me."

When the donation was announced, initiative proponents were furious.

"You've got this rich, liberal woman who wants to educate her kids off of the backs of our kids by having our kids teach her child how to speak Spanish," said Rita Montero, chairwoman of English for the Children. "She's sort of like a vampire, sucking blood out of our kids and walking away with a smile on her face."

The day after the announcement, the ad blitz began. With Stryker's money, English Plus was able to mount a $2.9 million media campaign (a figure roughly equal to the entire budget for Governor Bill Owens, who was on the ballot at the same time).

The *Rocky Mountain News* described the Stryker-funded ads as "dark, showing still pictures of sad-looking children while an announcer ominously lists the faults in Amendment 31. In one, the announcer states that children who speak little English, largely Hispanic students, would disrupt the education of 'your children'—presumably the majority white families of Colorado."

While the ads were denounced as "ugly," Welchert had his eye on defeating Amendment 31. "Yeah, it's ominous," he told the *Rocky Mountain News*, "but it's cutting through." Polls bore out Welchert's appraisal. An October survey, conducted after the Stryker-funded advertisements began to run, showed support dropping like a rock.

Gully Stanford, cochairman of English Plus, told the *Rocky Mountain News* that Amendment 31's slide was about more than money. He cited the fact that the popular Republican governor Owens had announced his opposition to the initiative. "People are responding to our message," he said, "not the money."

The author of the initiative, Ron Unz, had a different view. "The opponents in Colorado did pretty much exactly what the opponents did in Massachusetts, and in California and in Arizona," he told the *Rocky Mountain News*. "The only difference was the massive amount of advertising on the 'No' side, 99 percent funded by a billionaire heiress named Pat Stryker." Unz later estimated that his side had been outspent by a margin of 15–1.

In the end, the initiative failed by a vote of 56 percent to 44 percent.

Less than a year later, Yates approached Stryker with a proposition even more ambitious than defeating a ballot initiative: did she want to help flip control of the state from Republican to Democrat?

Stryker said yes.

With her resources and interest in progressive politics, Stryker welcomed the chance to work with strategists who had the energy and vision to transform her state. She was fond of quoting Harry S. Truman's line that "it's amazing what you can accomplish if you don't care who gets the credit."

Stryker wasn't after glory. She just wanted to change Colorado.

Yates arranged meetings for Stryker and fellow donors, potential candidates, political operatives, and elected officials. Each Saturday in the fall of 2003, Yates, Jared Polis, and then Colorado attorney general (and current secretary of the interior) Ken Salazar met with prominent Democratic officeholders to discuss a comprehensive strategy for 2004. Consensus formed around the need for good candidates, good messages, and enough money to fund a first-rate operation.

Stryker was ready to give whatever it took to win. As the minivan-driving billionaire would tell anyone who questioned her commitment, "You never give someone half a life preserver."

Chapter Three

Rutt Bridges:
Political Nonprofits and the
Architecture of Change

Most Denverites can't point you to the Wells Fargo Center. But ask the way to the "cash register building" and you'll get a knowing nod and a gesture in the direction of the most iconic modern structure on the Denver skyline. The building's signature curved roof, created by architect Philip Johnson, is heated to prevent snow from sliding off its crown during the winter and spring. Home to banks, law firms, and a mining company, it's the most visible property in downtown Denver.

In 1999, the Wells Fargo Center became home to a different kind of tenant. The Bighorn Center for Public Policy wouldn't last a decade (it closed in 2006), but in its few short years of existence it became a model of how nonprofit entities could influence the political dynamics of a state.

Inside Suite 2000, everyone who came through the center's doors was measured up. Not just for their intellectual acumen, but actually measured by height with a pencil against one of the walls. In 2003, there were a couple of Republican politicians (former Wyoming US senator Alan Simpson and Colorado state senator Ken Chlouber) who held the distinction for looking down on many of their counterparts, literally speaking.

Well under six feet tall, Rutt Bridges didn't register on the wall, but his stature was felt everywhere else in the office. He spent $1 million of his own money creating the nonprofit in 1999 with the purpose of giving "Colorado's political middle a credible and legitimate voice in the state's increasingly polarized landscape and, more importantly, to get things done."

He filled his board with some of the state's biggest political players from both major parties, focusing specifically on people whose successes in life were rooted in education. On the Democratic side, he brought to the table former governor Richard Lamm and former US senator Gary Hart, both intellectual heavyweights.

For Republican perspective, he reached out to Ed McVaney, who struggled with dyslexia as a child before earning an undergraduate degree in mechanical engineering and a master's degree in business administration. McVaney created JD Edwards, revolutionized business and accounting software development, and became a major supporter of Republican causes.

Steve Schuck taught math and coached football after college before moving to the Colorado Springs area and turning a small real estate firm into a major developer of billions of dollars worth of commercial and residential projects. Schuck, at the time the foremost advocate for school choice in the region, supported many Republican candidates in the process.

Bridges respected hard work, starting from when he was nine years old and took his first job helping his father drill mud pits for water wells in rural Georgia.

He excelled in physics at the Georgia Institute of Technology (Georgia Tech) and then, after receiving a master's degree in geophysics, took a job at Chevron, where he started building his own microcomputer.

When the energy giant wasn't interested in creating "toys," Bridges moved to Denver, set up his own company, and revolutionized the industry. His surveying software created three-dimensional computer images of underground oil and gas deposits, giving companies a significant advantage in knowing where they should drill.

After selling his company for "more money than I could spend in my life," Bridges became hooked on politics. He sold his concept to politicians, donors, and the media with words like *civil* and *rational* and highlighted their differences from the bickering and partisanship currently associated with the system.

The emergence of Bridges's vision through Bighorn coincided with legal changes to campaign finance laws that would, in time, shift the center of political power away from candidates and campaigns and toward independent nonprofits whose funding sources are often hidden from the public. Although Bighorn was founded before these laws would change the political landscape, it was perfectly positioned to become a relevant force in Colorado politics once the rules of the game changed.

And soon they did.

In 2002, Congress passed McCain-Feingold, which restricted the amount of money federal candidates could raise from donors. That same year, Colorado citizens enacted Amendment 27, a constitutional amendment that capped state legislative contributions at $400 per donor and statewide candidate contributions (such as governor, treasurer, and secretary of state) at $1,000. Authored by the nonprofit Common Cause, Amendment 27 effectively took message control out of the hands of candidates and handed it to outsiders.

"Common Cause knew exactly what they were doing," said former Colorado Republican Party executive director Alan Philp. "Amendment 27 gave a systematic advantage to Democrats by limiting the participation of a key group of Republican donors: those in the $1,000 to $25,000 range. That sounds like a lot, but in real terms those are actually medium-sized donors. After Amendment 27, the only people who could make a big difference were super-rich donors—those who can give $100,000 or more to outside groups—and labor unions, who got special loopholes under the new rules."

After Amendment 27, campaign spending in meaningful quantities could only be accomplished through the "independent sector"—a collection of nonprofit organizations that stepped into the role once occupied by political parties. In time, the seeds sown at Bighorn would grow into a garden of think tanks, political 527s, 501(c)(3) charitable organizations, 501(c)(4) "social welfare" organizations, new media outlets, progressive watchdog groups, and assorted activist organizations that would play a key role in the political transformation of Colorado from 2004 to 2008.

Speaking to a group of lawyers in Denver in 2008, Democratic attorney Mark Grueskin summed up the new reality of political giving: "With the increased imposition of contribution limits, political money finds a way to the political system—always does, always has...And those of you in this room are simply among the blessed, because you get to help people give politically. They're going to give. And now they do it through nonprofit entities."

The cost of participation in elections through the independent sector is high, especially at the state level. Political nonprofits are subject to byzantine tax, corporate, and accounting rules and require constant guidance from lawyers and accountants. That guidance is expensive, which is why there's no such thing as a mom-and-pop political nonprofit. Small and medium donors need not apply.

Bridges's financial resources gave him the ability to build a thriving independent sector organization in short order. Bighorn was actually two organizations, not one. The first, the Bighorn Center for Public Policy, was a charitable organization organized under Section 501(c)(3) of the federal tax code. Under federal law, 501(c)(3)s (or "C3s," as they're often called) may only promote a limited number of activities, including charitable, religious, educational, scientific, or literary pursuits. To preserve their tax-exempt status,

501(c)(3)s are, according to the Internal Revenue Service (IRS), "absolutely prohibited from participating in, or intervening in, any political campaign on behalf of (or in opposition to) any candidate for elective public office."

To remain politically effective without compromising its tax-exempt status, Bighorn defined its mission narrowly. "The concept [is] to bring together leaders from both parties, good ideas (best practices) from other states, the private sector, and to use objective data and research in order to identify, develop, and advocate public policies that improve the lives of Coloradans," its website stated. "As part of the mission, the Bighorn Center actively recruits and trains leaders who share these values through a bipartisan leadership development program."

The second Bighorn organization was Bighorn Action, organized under Section 501(c)(4) of the federal tax code, which regulates what the IRS calls "social welfare organizations." Whereas 501(c)(3)s are charitable in nature, 501(c)(4)s are given more latitude under law to engage in issue advocacy, which can and often does bleed into political activities. More importantly, 501(c)(4)s are allowed to engage in election activities, as long as they are related to the organization's purpose.

The two Bighorn entities worked side by side to accomplish a variety of goals. The think tank worked on bipartisan issues at the Capitol such as suicide prevention, anti-bullying, fiscal reform, sentencing reform for drug offenders, disclosure of political advertising, creating a rainy-day fund in the state budget, and pre-school funding.

Bighorn Action aggressively promoted issues that were directly related to campaigns and elections, such as campaign finance reform, voter registration, mail voting, and ballot access for candidates.

Bighorn's biggest success was to help pass legislation that created Colorado's telemarketer no-call list, making cold calls to residents illegal. The Republican sponsor, Senator Chlouber, called the measure "Colorado common sense," saying that "no one wanted to get a call in the middle of dinner from a sales guy in New Jersey offering everything from aluminum siding to an autographed picture of Jesus Christ."

The media ate it up, and Bridges found himself doing numerous interviews on the topic. To show lawmakers how popular the concept was, Bighorn created its own no-call list, intending to turn over the numbers to the state if the legislation was passed. Hundreds of thousands of residents signed up.

"We want to find a way to give people back the privacy of their homes," Bridges often said.

Within months of Governor Bill Owens signing the bill into law, Bighorn's hundreds of thousands of Coloradans had turned into millions of Coloradans asking that they not be called by telemarketers. One consumer reporter in Denver labeled it the "most meaningful, most impactful piece of consumer legislation passed in Colorado in twenty-five years."

The success fueled Bridges's belief that "issues

that have great practical impact on the lives of all Coloradans should not be held hostage to political bickering." And yet at the Capitol, bickering over what leading Democrats and even some Republicans called "God, guns, and gays" dominated the headlines at a time when the state was facing a massive budget deficit.

To the consternation of Democrats, Republican legislative leadership was focused on a plan to promote "intellectual diversity" in classes and faculty recruiting, citing concerns that students were being exposed only to liberal philosophies from their professors and, worse, could be penalized for expressing conservative beliefs in the classroom. Bridges, meanwhile, worried there wouldn't be anyone in those classrooms because the state had cut financial aid. He thought Republicans' priorities were misguided.

"I grew up in poor circumstances," he later told a reporter. "Then I went to Georgia Tech. That was my ticket out."

"When you look at the promise of America, a big piece of it is people believing they can better themselves through education. The ability to get a college education with reasonable tuition is part of government. There are reasons as a society we support public functions. We seem to be losing that."

"Higher ed was being slashed, and while higher ed was being slashed, they were talking about purging liberal faculty members," Jared Polis later said. "These things may appeal to their base, but they were not taking on the issues that faced Colorado. That's one of the things that drove me to the table. I know for Rutt that was a big part of it, [too]. The Republican leadership just seemed asleep at the wheel."

"They were off talking about liberals in higher education rather than funding higher education, which really angered Rutt," said Polis. "This is what was going on."

Bridges started to kick around the idea of his own run for office and in February 2004 announced his candidacy for the US Senate against the Republican incumbent, Senator Ben Nighthorse Campbell.

"Everyone here who knows me," he said during the campaign kickoff, "knows that I am not a professional politician, I'm a businessman. I haven't spent my life courting special interest[s]. I haven't spent my life pretending that I have all the answers. I'm running for this office because I'm tired of the grip partisan ideologies, both Democrat and Republican, have on this government."

Less than a week later, Campbell stepped out of the race, citing health reasons. Colorado's more established politicians on both sides entertained running for the office. For the Republicans, Owens and then US representatives Scott McInnis and Tom Tancredo passed. For the Democrats, Representative Mark Udall committed to the race briefly before Attorney General Ken Salazar announced his candidacy.

Bridges himself exited the race a mere ten days later, praising Salazar as an individual who "has always been about both sides working together for the good of Colorado."

With no office to run for, Bridges still wanted to make a difference, he just didn't know how or where.

In hindsight, Bridges was able to make more of a difference behind the scenes than he could as a candidate. The reason was right under his nose. Although the 501(c)(3) think tank grabbed headlines with the no-call list and other public policy initiatives, in the 501(c)(4) Bighorn Action, Bridges created a template for using nonprofit organizations to influence elections.

In time, political nonprofits would do more than just influence elections. They would tip the balance of power at the state Capitol.

Chapter Four

Tim Gill: "Somebody's Gotta Go"

The House Education Committee was running late. After-lunch hearings tended to start on LST (legislative standard time) anyway, but today was worse than usual. The committee meeting had been moved from its traditional spot in the basement of the state Capitol, and those who hadn't paid attention to the calendar hurried to catch one of the building's two painfully slow elevators. Some gave up, opting to jog up two flights of Colorado-quarried-marble stairs to the Old Supreme Court Chambers.

Committee members hustled through the dark hallways, weaving through the throng of lobbyists, reporters, and members of the public, into the sunlit room. Stately, and nearly two stories high, it was by far the largest hearing room in the Capitol, typically set aside for controversial and high-profile events that promised to attract large crowds.

And the first bill on the committee's agenda for March 15, 2004, was nothing if not controversial.

The committee's chair, Representative Nancy Spence, a Republican from Centennial, had told her colleagues to beware the ides of March. She was expecting one of the more "divisive" debates in recent memory. Two hundred people filled the room, looking up at the eleven-member committee seated behind the ornate wooden bench on the dais at the front of the room, waiting to hear testimony and discussion about House Bill 1375.

The bill would prohibit a "school district from providing instruction relating to sexual lifestyles that are alternative to heterosexual relationships, except in the context of instruction concerning the risk and prevention of sexually transmitted disease." It had been controversial since being introduced almost a month earlier. Some called it homophobic, others labeled it prudent. Today, at last, the bill would be heard in an open public forum.

The setting was impressive. After eighty-five years of smoky hearings, the room's finely crafted woodwork, carved plaster ceilings, and one-ton chandelier had been restored. Maroon drapes covered windows at either end of the dais and served as the background for a marble bust of Colorado's first chief justice, Henry C. Thatcher.

High above the committee members were seven stained-glass panels honoring members of four ethnic groups that had impacted Colorado history. One depicted Naoichi "Harry" Hokazono, who became a leading businessman at the beginning of the nineteenth century and helped create massive infrastructure projects, such as the Moffat Tunnel, which cut through the Continental Divide in north-central Colorado.

Sitting in the audience, almost completely unnoticed that day, was another Coloradan who was living the American dream.

Tim Gill grew up in the suburbs west of Denver, the son of a plastic surgeon and a homemaker. Smart, analytical, and with a passion for science fiction, he went to the University of Colorado in 1972, where he became interested in the fledgling field of computer science. After earning a degree in applied mathematics in 1976, he went to work developing computer software for ALF Products and Hewlett Packard.

As Gill's acumen with technological processes grew, so did the computer industry. In 1981, he decided to strike out on his own with a modest loan of $2,000 from his parents. They "never thought they'd see the money again," he told *Denver Magazine* in 2008. But they did, and sooner than they expected: Gill repaid the loan in full within a month.

During the 1980s, Gill built his start-up, Quark, Inc., into a software giant. The company, which specialized in text-processing products, had its biggest score in 1987, when it released its desktop publishing software Quark XPress. By 1996, Gill was worth more than $400 million.

Computers were not the only thing Gill discovered as an undergraduate back in the 1970s. Within months of arriving on campus, he came out as a gay man. He also began what would become a lifelong fight for gay rights. Having protested courses that taught that homosexuality was a personality disorder, it seemed only natural that Gill would find himself in a hearing room in 2004, waiting for the debate over House Bill 1375.

Yet it took more than a decade of growing

frustration to bring Gill to the Capitol, where he could finally engage the political process face-to-face.

Gill's journey to activism began in 1992. That year, 53.4 percent of the state's voters approved Amendment 2, a ballot measure excluding gays and lesbians from antidiscrimination laws, in the process nullifying ordinances in Denver, Aspen, and Boulder. National gay and lesbian organizations labeled Colorado the "hate state," organizing boycotts of Colorado products, such as Celestial Seasonings tea and Coors beer. A legal challenge eventually made its way to the US Supreme Court, which struck down Amendment 2 on constitutional grounds by a 6–3 vote.

To Gill, Amendment 2 was an unprovoked slap in the face for gay Coloradans. "Nothing can compare to the psychological trauma of realizing that more than half the people in your state believe that you don't deserve equal rights," he said in a 2000 interview with *The Chronicle of Philanthropy*.

"He's got one of the great American success stories and yet really, after Amendment 2, he was excluded from that story," said Sean Duffy, a Republican political consultant and friend of Gill. "He wasn't able to share in that success. He was labeled as substandard, if you will."

Gill was upset, and his business success enabled him to do something about it. In 1993, he pledged $1 million "to raise awareness in Colorado about the effects of discrimination." Then, in 1994, he started the Gill Foundation with an endowment in excess of $200 million.

The Gill Foundation was not an overtly Democratic organization; in fact, it wasn't political at all. Organized as a charitable entity under section 501(c)(3) of the Internal Revenue Code, its stated purpose was "to secure equal opportunity for all people regardless of sexual orientation or gender expression." As a tax-exempt charity, it was (and is) prohibited by law from participating in partisan political activities. Instead, it focused on providing seed money for gay-rights organizations throughout the country. Since 1994, it has made about 250 grants annually, with awards ranging from $2,500 to $100,000 and averaging about $16,000. By one estimate, the Gill Foundation has given over $80 million to gay and lesbian causes since its inception.

In 1996, Gill expanded his mission and founded the Gay & Lesbian Fund for Colorado, which "supports nonprofit organizations in Colorado that are working to advance equality for all people, and additionally works to highlight the contributions of gay, lesbian, bisexual, and transgender people." Also organized as a 501(c)(3), the fund avoided overtly political activities, instead focusing on grants.

Headquartered in Colorado Springs, the Gay & Lesbian Fund gives about 250 grants annually (averaging about $7,000 each) and has given tens of millions of dollars to nonprofits throughout the state, ranging from symphonies and museums to health and well-being programs. One of the only requirements is that the applicant organization must have a "board-approved nondiscrimination statement that

includes sexual orientation and gender expression."
As the fund articulates to all applicants, "Colorado
will realize its full potential when everyone has an
opportunity for equality."

Through the 1990s and into the 2000s, Gill's
efforts were more philanthropic than political. According to *The Atlantic*, in 2000 he gave $300,000 in
political contributions, and in 2002 he gave $800,000.
Large numbers, to be sure, but only a fraction of his
giving as a whole. Nor were his dollars solely directed
to Democrats—as late as 2003 he gave $10,000 to the
Republican Governors Association. Years later, he
said, "I've never believed Republicans are inherently
antigay. Republicans, Democrats, and independents
all want to make the world a better place, but that
has to include equality for gay, lesbian, bisexual, and
transgender people."

For all his wealth and inclination toward social
change, until 2004 Gill's giving had been heavily
tilted toward foundations, grants, and white papers—
not candidates and campaigns.

On March 15, 2004, that would change. Gill
was about to make the big leap from philanthropy to
politics.

Gill's newly awakened interest in politics was good
news to Ted Trimpa, who sat next to Gill in the Old
Supreme Court Chambers. Although the lobbyist and
political consultant was only thirty-seven, he had

made a name for himself in the corridors of power at the state Capitol. But as a Democrat, Trimpa's influence was limited by the fact that Republicans controlled both the legislature and the governor's office.

Trimpa's life experience set him apart from most Denver Democrats. "Deep down, Ted is a farm kid," said former GOP strategist J. J. Ament, who also has rural roots. Trimpa's hometown of Sublette, Kansas (named for French fur trader and western pioneer William Lewis Sublette), isn't on any tourist maps. With a population of 1,592, it is located just a little north of the center of the geographic triangle formed by Pueblo, Colorado, Wichita, Kansas, and Amarillo, Texas.

In high school, Trimpa was an extrovert and a leader. The two-time Kansas state debate champion played the sousaphone in the high school marching band and at halftime would transform himself into the Lark, Sublette's mascot, cracking up the home crowd as he chased the opposing team's cheerleaders with a toilet plunger.

When the school year ended, work began. For most American kids, summer vacation means time off—sports camps, family trips, and afternoons spent by the swimming pool. Not for Trimpa. Seven days a week, he was up at 4:30 AM to check irrigation wells with his father on the family farm, where they raised corn, wheat, and cattle. Before the sun came up, Trimpa had done more than most kids his age did all day.

Yet, growing up, Trimpa had a secret. From the sixth grade on, he knew he was gay. But Trimpa didn't dare come out—not in Sublette. That was unthink-able. So he dutifully played the part of the straight kid. "I wasn't much of a prom date, I'm afraid," he laughs now. "But at least my tie always matched her dress."

By the time Trimpa enrolled at the University of Denver, in 1985, his secret was starting to eat away at him—literally. He had painful ulcers. He abhorred himself for having impure thoughts. He figured if he prayed harder, worked harder, fought harder, he could overcome this problem. But nothing seemed to have any effect.

When he entered the University of Denver College of Law, in 1990, Trimpa's problems had gone from bad to worse. He plunged into depression. His grades went off a cliff. He gained weight. Hoping for respite, he tried antidepressants and sought psychological help. "Somewhere in Denver there's a therapist driving a [BMW] 7 Series that I paid for," he says now.

In retrospect, Trimpa found the cure for all his ailments so obvious: on February 19, 1991, he told a friend he was gay. Instantly, the physical and mental turmoil just went away. "It was a relief not to be fighting myself every day," he said later. "I could be myself for the first time in my life."

Trimpa's revelation, however, did not go over well at home. In August 1993, he gathered his parents in the large kitchen of the farmhouse in Sublette and broke the news. His mother started shaking. His father cried. From that time, things would never be the same.

Trimpa's father made it clear that he could still come home for holidays, as long as he came alone.

Not wanting to choose between his family and the man he was in a relationship with, one year Trimpa arranged to have a split Christmas. He and his partner stayed at his sister's house, where they celebrated Christmas together. Then Trimpa drove across town and celebrated for a second time with his parents. It was tense, awkward, and disastrous.

After that, Trimpa and his parents managed to coexist in the realm between détente and total estrangement. He talked to his mother occasionally, his father rarely, and never again tried to go home for the holidays. By the time his father died, in 1999, Trimpa had reconciled himself to being on his own.

In Denver, Trimpa built a new life for himself. When his grandmother cut off his funds for law school, he sought work at a Denver lobbying firm. "Are you willing to work for tobacco companies?" asked Frank "Pancho" Hays III, an influential Denver lobbyist. Trimpa said yes—he needed the money.

In the years he worked for Hays, Trimpa earned a reputation for being a brilliant strategist and effective tactician. "Ted thinks ten steps down the line," said Ament. "When he takes move number one, he knows what move number ten will be. He's very practical."

Among his friends, Trimpa also came to be known for his garden, which he keeps on the roof of his Denver penthouse apartment. He keeps artichokes, grapes, lilies, strawberries, dahlias, a pear tree, a cherry tree, and the occasional experimental plant. Once, a friend bet Trimpa he couldn't grow peanuts in the dry, high-plains climate. Six months later, he saw the friend at a bar. Reaching into his pocket, Trimpa pulled out a small handful of peanuts and tossed them onto a table. "You lose," he said.

Trimpa learned the art of horticulture from his grandmother, after whom a hybrid daylily—the Wilma Trimpa—is named. He learned to be patient and exacting. He learned to alter his methods when a plan didn't work the first time. He learned to be flexible. "It takes time and persistence to make something grow, especially in a harsh environment," he said. "If you rush it, it'll die."

This quality of patience would, in time, prove invaluable to the coalition-building at the heart of the Democratic turnaround in Colorado. In the coming years, Trimpa would help bring together a variety of progressive interest groups who had never effectively coalesced around a common goal. Often, Trimpa was the glue that held them together.

Trimpa also brought another critical quality to the table: unlike many of his Democratic allies, Trimpa understood Republicans. Between college and law school, he worked on the Washington staff of former US senator Nancy Kassebaum (R-KS). He had a good read on the art of the possible in Colorado's conservative-leaning political environment, especially when it came to promoting a gay rights agenda.

"We have got to be careful about expecting people overnight to understand what it is like to be gay," Trimpa told the *Bay Area Reporter* in 2006. "It took me over twelve years to come to grips with the fact that I was gay...And we're expecting people in a shorter period of time—when you think about real public awareness of gay rights—just to do that overnight. I don't think that is fair."

Yet, for all his pragmatism, Trimpa was never afraid to play hardball. Called "Colorado's answer to Karl Rove" by *The Atlantic*, Trimpa believes that to win, you need to go negative. "You have to create an environment of fear and respect," he told the *Bay Area Reporter*. "The only way to do that is to get aggressive and go out and actually beat them up [politically]. Sitting there crying and whining about it isn't going to get us equality. What is going to get us equality is fighting for it."

Trimpa knew that equality for gays and lesbians would begin at the state legislature. "Ted understood that there needed to be changes in the legislature to move a more progressive agenda," said Lynne Mason of the Colorado Education Association. That meant electing Democrats and defeating Republicans.

Trimpa was ready to fight the Colorado Republican Party. He was hoping that after today's hearing on House Bill 1375, Gill would be ready too.

At 2:23 PM the gavel dropped.

Almost immediately, the bill's sponsor, Representative Shawn Mitchell, a Republican from the northern suburbs of Denver, proposed an amendment. The new language would no longer mention homosexuality, and it wouldn't ban teachers from discussing it. Instead, it would simply require schools to notify parents and provide them with details on classes addressing human sexuality, along with a parental right to opt a child out of the class without penalty.

Despite the proposed amendment, however, the die had been cast. The testimony over the next three hours was all about homosexuality.

Gays make up only 2 percent to 10 percent of the population, said Representative Mitchell, and therefore should not have their wishes imposed upon the majority of students. He introduced mothers such as Kim Middaugh, who had three children in the Boulder Valley School District, and who was worried about a "secret" campaign with "pro-homosexuality teaching" to make kids in elementary school sympathetic to gays and lesbians.

Another parent of three, Debbie Liskey, said, "Parents are not being informed about what their kids are learning at school...We should have sex education in schools, but I don't think children should hear how sex is performed."

A Democratic representative asked Mitchell why celibacy and abstinence didn't constitute "alternative sexual lifestyles."

He countered that his proposal, which also called for parents to be given permission slips if their child was to be learning about sex education, was empowering to parents, not discriminatory toward gays. "This is expanding the opportunity of parents to be aware of what information is going into their children's minds and hearts," he said.

After testimony from more than two dozen people, the bill was amended as recommended by Mitchell. It then passed on a 6–5 party-line vote, with all the Republicans in favor and the Democrats opposed.

The bill had been watered down considerably, but to Gill it didn't matter. He had seen what Trimpa wanted him to see.

On their way out of the hearing room, Gill and Trimpa ran into Representative Alice Madden, a Democrat from Boulder.

"Tell Alice your new motto," Trimpa said to Gill.

The tall multimillionaire turned to the legislator and said, "Somebody's gotta go."

Part Two
The Plan

Chapter Five

Bringing It All Together:
The Roundtable Is Born

The Colorado Education Association (CEA) is the state's largest and most powerful teacher's union. Sitting across the street from the Capitol, the CEA's gray, four-story headquarters building is a powerful presence for the organization that represents 38,500 public sector jobs.

The Columbine Room, near the first-floor entrance to the building, is fairly nondescript as conference rooms go—the exposed concrete decor is dated, the carpet drab, the fluorescent lighting pale and lacking in natural colors. Even the students in the photos adorning the walls have probably long since graduated from high school and now have kids of their own.

But in the summer of 2004, the Columbine Room became the ultimate smoke-free backroom of Colorado politics.

For the past year, multimillionaires Jared Polis, Pat Stryker, Tim Gill, and Rutt Bridges had been gearing up to get involved in legislative elections. They held parallel conversations, each trying to find the best way to make a difference. In 2003, Al Yates and Stryker reached out to Polis and Bridges, dining with each on separate occasions. In April 2004, Yates met with Trimpa for a lunch that established the connection between Stryker and Gill. One month later,

Yates and Stryker took Stryker's private jet to meet with Gill at his Aspen home, where they discussed transforming Colorado politics. Afterward, Yates, Bridges, and Polis met in Fort Collins over dinner. In time, isolated one-on-one conversations became group meetings involving more players with more access to resources.

Everyone wanted to knock out the Republican monopoly at the Capitol. To that end, the donors, Bridges, Gill, Polis, and Stryker—who would later be dubbed the "Gang of Four" by the Colorado press—agreed to pool their resources in pursuit of that objective. By the summer of 2004, they were ready to give money on a level never before seen in Colorado politics.

The first order of business was to find field generals to coordinate the effort.

Lynne Mason was the political director and government relations specialist at the CEA. She lobbied lawmakers year in and year out to increase funding for K–12 education. "Our agenda was always about improving public education's standing in the state budget and the legislature," she said. But the Republican legislature never delivered as much money as she wanted.

She reached out to friends like Beth Ganz, who was in charge of Colorado's branch of the National Abortion Rights Action League (NARAL); Tony Massaro, who ran Colorado Conservation Voters (CCV); Steve Adams, who represented the American Federation of Labor—Congress of Industrial Organizations

(AFL-CIO); and Jennifer Brandeberry, who represented the Colorado Trial Lawyers Association (CTLA). Each organization had its own campaign capacities and membership lists, and they knew how to run get-out-the-vote and mail programs in state legislative races. They all wanted the Democrats to gain seats in the upcoming election.

That summer, the group began to gather for weekly meetings in the Columbine Room. Joining them were Ted Trimpa and Yates (who represented Gill and Stryker, respectively); progressive attorney and activist Michael Huttner; Bridges; Polis; state House assistant minority leader Alice Madden; Colorado Senate minority leader Joan Fitz-Gerald; and staff members and field coordinators Brandon Hall, Jill Hanauer, Anne Barkis, Paul Lhevine, and Tyler Chafee.

And so the Roundtable was born.

None of the participants remembers an "ah-ha" moment, no one specific meeting, where it all came together. When they started communicating, they had no clue what kind of an impact they could have. They just started communicating, and things went from there.

"We really didn't truly know how big this would become," said Polis. "Clearly, when we started, we had no idea. I didn't know this would have great historical significance, nor did anybody there, that we would transform Colorado. 'Let's get together and maybe we can flip the State Senate,' that's what we were thinking."

As the group began its regular meetings, there was always a cheese plate from Whole Foods, courtesy of Polis. "We started calling it the cheese group," recalled Polis with a grin. "We offered them cheese to get them there."

Cheese may have brought them there, but shared purpose and a growing sense of trust kept them coming back. Leaders soon emerged. "Lynne Mason's role cannot be [overstated]," said Hanauer. "She brought the intelligence, the logistics, and the [CEA] pocketbook to the group. She wasn't driven by partisan concerns; they were issue concerns around education and teachers. Everybody in that room, they weren't necessarily vitriolic Democrats. It was really about priorities."

Discussion of issues that might divide the group was strictly verboten. "All the participants checked their political agendas at the door," said Polis later. "There was never any policy discussed. There were never any issues discussed. This was simply a group of people who believed that all of our issues, and regardless of what they were, what our differences were, would be better represented in a Democratic majority."

NARAL's Ganz agreed. "The basic concept was simple," she said. "A group of people and organizations that didn't like the direction the state was moving in came together to try to win elections so that policies that were being promoted by the state legislature and the governor actually shifted. The execution of that was the challenge. Although, it didn't seem challenging because the goal of those who came together—winning elections—was the same."

They were all tired of losing. They wanted to win.

"To the extent there were arguments, they would always be tactical, about this race versus that race or what message to have," said Polis. But disagreements never derailed the group's efforts. They simply worked through their issues and moved forward.

Trimpa, who attended meetings as Gill's representative, kept Roundtable discussions focused on the task at hand. "[Ted is] very smart and strategic and he gets along with everybody," recalled Mason. "He's a good listener. He has all the qualities to lead. He brought knowledge, focus, strategic thinking, resources." Like the master gardener he is, Trimpa was attentive to the needs of each entity in the room, and he saw to it they were addressed.

But once the conversation was over, Trimpa was all action. As Mason said, "When Ted is in a room, he isn't afraid to be quiet and listen, but he also isn't afraid to jump in, say, 'Okay, we've talked about this enough. It's time to make a decision.'"

The group immediately recognized that campaign finance reform had completely changed the rules of the game. By limiting the amount of money candidates and political parties could raise and spend, the new law had seriously weakened candidates—and all but killed political parties.

"In the past, the party ran this whole apparatus, they called it the 'coordinated campaign,'" said Polis. "The party chairs were largely responsible for the fund-raising. The candidates helped raise money for the parties. It all went into one pot." After campaign finance reform, that pot shrunk to the size of a tea-cup. Polis knew that campaign finance reform "basically guaranteed that the party itself, Republican or Democrat, could not possibly be the main entity that...ran campaigns. The biggest thing is it took parties out of the mix as a money entity."

The vacuum left by the diminishment of the Colorado Democratic Party also created a tremendous opportunity for the Roundtable. Everyone knew the party had been notoriously inefficient when it came to spending its money. In Polis's view, this was a function of how people get into decision-making roles in state political parties. Party leaders "were selected because they travel the state," he observed. "They know people. They show up at every dinner. People like them. They manage the palace intrigues effectively."

But that was also a weakness. Applying a businessman's eye for organizational effectiveness, Polis identified what he believed was the main problem with political parties. "There's no reason to think [party leaders] would be good at running campaigns and making tough decisions...In fact, to the contrary. They would have a tendency to put valuable resources into races they're probably not going to win because they want to win friends. So, if they like so-and-so and they're running in a very Republican district, they're going to give them help, which takes it away from a very competitive district. So it wasn't a very good way to allocate resources."

The people at the Roundtable recognized that they, for all intents and purposes, *were* the party.

And that wasn't such a bad thing. For one thing, they didn't have to carry the "old" party's baggage. They wouldn't allow themselves to be caught up in inter-personal politics, nor would the multimillionaires (three of whom were self-made) tolerate undisci-plined spending. Everyone had a common goal and it wasn't to win friends. It was to win elections. That was the measure by which they would succeed or fail.

To fill the structural void created by the loss of the state Democratic Party, each member of the Round-table contributed his or her unique tools to the group's growing toolbox. NARAL and the trial lawyers tapped their donor networks to raise money for Democratic candidates. CEA had access to over a quarter of a mil-lion dollars in dues collected from its members, as well as an extensive membership list from which it acti-vated volunteers to turn out the vote on Election Day.

The AFL-CIO took advantage of a loophole in campaign finance law allowing labor unions to raise up to $50.00 per year from each of their members into "small donor committees"—which were, in turn, allowed to give ten times more in hard money contributions (i.e., direct donations) to candidates than any other donor. According to a 2005 study by Wayne State University, Colorado labor "played a big role in hard money donations to targeted candidates and accounted for over 50 percent of the hard dollar donations in five targeted Senate races and ten tar-geted House races, raising over $400,000."

Colorado Conservation Voters, which kept track of the votes of sitting legislators, asserted that most targeted Republicans were antienvironmental, at least when measured by the methodology of CCV's scorecard. Of six targeted House Republican incumbents, only one, Bob Briggs, scored a respectable eighty-nine out of a possible one hundred; the remaining five averaged a dismal forty-three points. Of the ten targeted House races, CCV endorsed Democrats in nine (Briggs was the lone exception), along with all of the Democrats in targeted Senate races. With their press contacts and large list of members, CCV pushed these findings out into the environmentally inclined Colorado electorate.

All of these groups' organizational capacity had existed before 2004, to one degree or another. But that summer, the Roundtable had four brand-new power tools in its toolbox—Bridges, Gill, Polis, and Stryker.

With campaign finance reform, the Gang of Four couldn't give much money directly to candidates, so they looked to other avenues. And the most obvious were 527s. Named after the section of federal tax law under which they are regulated, 527s were not new, but until campaign finance reform laws were passed in 2002, they rarely played a significant role in elections, especially at the state level. The Roundtable changed that.

In hindsight, it's remarkable how quickly members of the Roundtable adapted to the new campaign finance reality. While national political groups were beginning to use 527s (the Swift Boat Veterans for Truth is a famous example from the same time frame), in 2004 it was unusual for state-based organizations to understand these exotic organizations and complex rules that governed them—much less master them to the point that they could be used effectively.

The Roundtable capitalized on a key provision of post-campaign finance reform election law, namely, that while nonprofits were no longer allowed to coordinate their activities with candidates or political parties, they were perfectly free to coordinate among themselves.

And coordinate they did.

Members of the Roundtable used four principal 527s: one for the House (Alliance for Colorado's Families), one for the Senate (Forward Colorado), and two for field operations (Coalition for a Better Colorado and Alliance for a Better Colorado).

Alliance for Colorado's Families listed its officers as Jill Hanauer, president, and Anne Barkis, secretary and treasurer. Public filings listed its purpose as "to provide activities designed to accept contributions or make expenditures for influencing or attempting to influence the selection, nomination, or appointment of individuals to any state or local public office or in a political organization which supports the ideals and philosophy of the association regarding governmental programs and policies of importance to Colorado's families." Regardless of what the form said, however, Alliance for Colorado's Families was run by state House assistant minority leader Alice Madden, a Democrat from Boulder. And its purpose was simple: to elect Democratic candidates to the House.

The Senate 527, Forward Colorado, did not make filings with the Internal Revenue Service, but secretary of state records indicate that its representative was Brandon Hall, the Democratic caucus director for the Senate Democrats. (Hall is currently campaign manager for US Senate majority leader Harry Reid). Forward Colorado's registered address was Ten Lakeside Lane, the same address as the Colorado Teamsters Local Union No. 455.

Another 527 was Coalition for a Better Colorado. Its president, secretary, and treasurer was listed as Paul Lhevine, and its purpose was "to research social, fiscal, and educational-related concerns of the citizens of the State of Colorado and to provide public reporting of these findings and their implications and to increase awareness of such concerns and of alternative avenues for engaging in civic processes to address them." This was a joint field operation to benefit both House and Senate candidates, and it ran paid phone banks, coordinated voter identification, sent some get-out-the-vote mail, and deployed paid walkers.

Finally, in addition to Coalition for a Better Colorado, there was a smaller field 527 called Alliance for a Better Colorado, which performed precisely the same functions as Coalition for a Better Colorado with only one exception: it received no money from the teachers union. This gave the Roundtable a tool to get out the vote against the few Republican candidates who had been endorsed by the CEA, while insulating the CEA from those races.

The four 527s became the focal point of the Roundtable's strategic efforts, and they were the principal avenue of participation by Bridges, Gill, Polis, and Stryker. On May 13, Gill gave Forward Colorado $200,000, which was followed one week later by a check from Stryker for $81,891. Bridges sent Coalition for a Better Colorado $30,000 eleven days later, and three weeks after that Stryker gave another $85,534.07 to Forward Colorado. Nine days later, she followed up with a $90,000 gift to Coalition for a Better Colorado, and a week later Polis sent $50,000 to Forward Colorado. The next day, Stryker added $125,000 to Alliance for Colorado's Families' war chest, and one week later she sent $75,000 more to Forward Colorado. This pattern went on all summer and into the fall, with checks for $30,000 here and $50,000 there hitting the 527 accounts with more regularity than biweekly paydays. On one single day in September, the four donors gave a combined total of $290,000 to Coalition for a Better Colorado.

One 527 staffer who had been dispatched to Fort Collins to pick up a check from Stryker called her husband to tell him that the check she was holding was big enough to buy a house.

In the end, the donors gave enough to the four 527s to buy a small neighborhood—or maybe just a building the size of the state Capitol. By the conclusion of the election cycle, Stryker had given over

$850,000; Gill nearly $775,000; and Polis and Bridges just over $400,000 each.

With such overwhelming resources in hand, it would have been understandable if the Roundtable decided to get involved in races with a higher profile than the state legislature. In 2004, Colorado was initially considered a battleground state in the presidential election, with George W. Bush polling well but John Kerry in striking distance. US senator Ben Nighthorse Campbell's retirement set up a contest between Democratic attorney general Ken Salazar and businessman Pete Coors. And on the state's Western Slope, an open congressional seat created a toss-up race between Democratic state representative John Salazar (Ken's brother) and Republican Greg Walcher, the former executive director of the Colorado Department of Natural Resources.

But rather than spread itself across all of the possible races on the ballot that year, the group decided to narrow its focus to House and Senate campaigns. "We're going to be the outside campaign group that works on the state legislative candidates," Polis recalled the group deciding.

A local focus was natural for the state-based unions and other interest groups at the Roundtable— their charge was to effect change at the state legislature. But in 2004, it was unusual anywhere in the United States for donors of the magnitude of the

Gang of Four to plow so many resources into down-ballot races.

In a 2007 interview with *The Atlantic*, Trimpa dismissed the tendency of big donors to focus on high-profile races as "glamour giving." He argued that "the temptation is always to swoon for the popular candidate, but a fraction of that money, directed at the right state and local races, could have flipped a few [state legislative] chambers."

More to the point, the state legislature—invisible as it was to most large donors—was the engine that drove most policy affecting gay rights, the cause closest to the hearts of Gill and Trimpa.

As *The Atlantic* noted, "Gill and Trimpa decided to eschew national races in favor of state and local ones, which could be influenced in large batches and for far less money. Most antigay measures, they discovered, originated in state legislatures." For Gill, that lesson had been learned in a Capitol hearing room just a few months earlier.

Polis pointed to another reason: control of the state legislature was low-hanging fruit, waiting to be plucked by the first group of big donors who recognized the opportunity.

"It's simpler than it sounds," he said. "These down-ballot races have enormous drop-off from the presidential tally, so there's no doubt about it. By building name recognition in down-ballot races, you can of course win seats that are majority on the other side. It's not even a matter necessarily of convincing [George W.] Bush voters to go for a Democrat, but it's a matter of convincing our voters to check off all the candidates down the line."

As the opportunity became clearer, people began to understand the potential upside of what they were doing. "We said, 'Why don't we do it together and be on the same page?'" Polis said. "Let's look at the races and decide which ones we want to target. All these entities had operated politically before this, but we'd never really talked to each other about it and coordinated."

By coordinating their efforts, members of the Roundtable stretched their dollars and eliminated duplicative efforts. Each resource was a separate tool in the toolbox, but everybody was in sync when it came to the overall blueprint. Everyone knew his or her place, and everyone was accountable to the group.

Decisions were driven by data. If data wasn't available, it was gathered. "We did it very scientifically," said Polis. "We looked at polling. We looked at messaging. We all looked at the mail pieces that went out. It was a very scrappy, get-it-done-type effort."

Throughout, the buzzword was *accountability*. "People too often measure activity rather than outcome," Roundtable member Huttner later told Brad Jones, who runs the conservative news organization Face the State. "Anybody, if they have the money, can make 9,000 phone calls and knock on 30,000 doors." But to the Roundtable, all that mattered was whether those calls and knocks on the doors affected the outcome of the election.

For Democrats, it was downright businesslike. "It's simple," said Polis. "You approach it with a business mentality. You say, 'Our goal is to establish a Democratic majority.' What's the best way to do that? Let's not talk about issues. Let's not talk about ego. They're all off the table."

"If you're in the room, it means you think a Democratic majority's going to be better for your beliefs," Polis recalled. "If you no longer believe that, fine, get out of the room."

Of the \$3.6 million raised by the Roundtable's 527s, nearly \$2.5 million—more than two-thirds—came from the Gang of Four. By contrast, in 2004 the Republican House and Senate 527s (there was no separate field organization) raised a combined total of \$845,000—all told, less than Stryker's individual contribution to the other side.

"We ran it like a business," Polis said.

Chapter Six

Money, Technology, and Shoe Leather: The Roundtable Builds a Ground Game

Lakeside Amusement Park sits alongside Lake Rhoda, one of the few natural bodies of water in metropolitan Denver. On warm summer nights, the shimmering light from hundreds of tiny bulbs adorning the Tower of Jewels, Lakeside's signature landmark, evokes the nostalgic past of the aging and genteelly shabby park.

Called "The Coney Island of the West" when it opened in 1908, its ballroom hosted the likes of Perry Como back in the day. Lakeside still boasts the Cyclone, one of the few remaining wooden roller coasters in the country.

Just a few feet from the lake, a miniature train station welcomes visitors to Puffing Billy and Whistling Tom, two four-foot eight-inch coal-burning steam trains that came from the 1904 World's Fair in Saint Louis. The track runs around the perimeter of the lake, past an enormous dirt parcel where a former shopping mall is being redeveloped into an office park.

Farther along, the track bends around the west side of the lake and makes its way back to the park, passing within a few feet of the wooden deck behind Ten Lakeside Lane, a nondescript, two-story brick building that faces the roar of Interstate 70.

It was in this building where the strategies hatched at the Roundtable were put into action.

The sign in front of Ten Lakeside Lane announces that this is the home of Teamsters Local 455. Suite 3A belongs to one of two Teamsters affiliates serving the Denver area. Just down the hall, in Suite 2A, is Teamsters Joint Council No. 3, serving working families from the Rocky Mountains to the Desert Southwest, territory from Idaho and Montana in the north to New Mexico and Arizona in the south and every state in between.

In the summer of 2004, Ten Lakeside Lane was also headquarters to Coalition for a Better Colorado, the Roundtable's field operation. The front line of the group's efforts, Coalition for a Better Colorado's purpose was to contact voters and gather information about them (also known as voter identification) using a combination of old-fashioned shoe leather and cutting-edge technology.

Coalition for a Better Colorado was a joint operation, meaning it would support the efforts of both the House and Senate 527s. In the early part of the summer, the Roundtable decided, the focus would be on the Colorado Senate, where Republicans clung to a tenuous 18–17 margin. It was their greatest opportunity, but also their greatest risk.

State Senate terms are four years, with roughly half of the Senate being up in any given election cycle. With only eighteen of the Senate's thirty-five seats in play in 2004, the playing field was narrow to begin with. Of those eighteen, four were solidly Republican and seven were solidly Democratic. Of the remaining seven, three leaned Republican, three leaned Democratic, and one—Senate District 14 in Fort Collins—was a true toss-up. The Democratic incumbent in Senate District 14, Peggy Reeves, was term limited, making way for a battle between Democratic state representative Bob Bacon and Republican Ray Martinez, the mayor of Fort Collins.

On paper, Democrats could hold their solid seats, hold the seats that leaned their way, and hold the toss-up seat in Fort Collins—and still end up on the short end of an 18–17 Senate. That meant they had to win at least one of the three seats that leaned Republican, all with Republican incumbents.

After evaluating available data, the Roundtable narrowed its focus to four districts: a rural district in northwest Colorado (held by incumbent Republican Jack Taylor), the open Fort Collins seat, and two seats in suburban Arapahoe County (held by incumbent Republican senators Jim Dyer and Bruce Cairns). In other words, to get to 18, Democrats would have to beat a popular Hispanic Republican mayor in his hometown and take out at least one incumbent Republican senator. But the Roundtable had a plan, and by the end of July, the Senate 527, Forward Colorado, had collected almost $500,000 from Tim Gill, Jared Polis, and Pat Stryker.

Although the Senate seemed winnable, the House, where Republicans held a comfortable 37–28 majority, looked tough: only twenty-two of the sixty-five districts had 50 percent or greater Democratic registration.

But House Minority caucus chair Alice Madden, who ran the House 527, Alliance for Colorado's Families, saw a path to victory when few others did.

"Initially, we were tilting at windmills," said Jill Hanauer, who worked with Representative Madden. "No one thought we could take the House."

But Madden believed.

She first became emboldened after an October 2003 meeting with Al Yates and Stryker in Fort Collins. Madden, House minority leader Andrew Romanoff, and Representative Angie Paccione had driven north of the Capitol to Fort Collins to pitch Yates and Stryker on their plans. They felt confident they would pick up one term-limited seat held by a Republican in a heavily Democratic district, but that meant they still needed four more to retake the majority.

Paccione nicknamed the quest the "Drive for Five," a reference to her college basketball career at Stanford. Madden had a PowerPoint presentation illustrating the five Republicans they would target, shared what little polling data they had, and challenged Yates and Stryker to become a part of history.

Yates looked at them and said, "Why settle for five? Why not target eight to ten?"

Yates's response was encouraging, but Madden still had work to do to convince other Roundtable members that it was worth spending some of the resources that would have gone to the Senate on the House. Polis was one of the skeptics. "We knew we'd flip the Senate," he recalled. "We were just one seat down and we felt pretty comfortable we would do it, but the House, we thought we'd pick up [just] a couple seats."

Madden and her team went back to the drawing board and came up with a plan.

Of the sixty-five House seats, all were up for reelection. Of those, only ten were truly competitive—and of those, two were held by incumbent Democrats and would need to be protected. Of the remaining eight, three were held by Republican incumbents and five were open seats that had been previously held by Republicans. The bottom line was that Democrats would have to win seven of the ten targeted seats to capture the majority.

The devil, however, was in the details: there was no way to make the math work without picking up Republican-leaning seats, and it would probably be necessary to defeat at least one incumbent Republican in the process. Because the races would be close, they would have to target all eight Republican seats and hope at least five went their way.

The scope of Madden's plan was unprecedented. It was so preposterously ambitious, so expensive, so over the top, it never even occurred to Republicans that it might happen. "Nobody thought the Democrats had the resources to take the House," said Rob Fairbank, at the time a GOP legislator from a western suburb of Denver.

But Madden believed.

Madden's House 527, Alliance for Colorado's Families, wrote up detailed plans for each of the targeted races, supported by polling and other research, setting forth budgets and strategies that would be necessary to win the seats. Each memo resembled the kind of business plan an entrepreneur seeking seed money might present to a venture capital fund—which was, in a sense, the role being played by the donors at the Roundtable.

One memo noted that a majority of voters in a conservative Grand Junction district thought Colorado was heading in the right direction, so "emphasizing change would undoubtedly be a mistake." Alliance for Colorado's Families recommended a campaign strategy that pointed to Democratic candidate Bernie Buescher's community service and "distinctive personal story." They targeted men under forty, women under fifty-five, and those with a college degree or less of education. They proposed a budget with $41,000 for television advertisements attacking Buescher's opponent and an additional $29,000 on field workers to pass out leaflets supporting Buescher.

In the western suburbs of Denver, Madden's candidate was Pete Mazula. He was a firefighter who had contracted hepatitis C while attempting to save someone's life on the job. His opponent was twenty-nine-year-old Matt Knoedler, "who has worked for Republican politicians all his adult life." The strategy called for eight mail pieces backed by $70,000 targeting 13,926 households and automated calls from firefighters and doctors that included celebrating Mazula's heroism and condemning the "typical Republican establishment candidate." Alliance for Colorado's Families recommended linking "him to the negative proposals performed by his bosses."

In the end, Madden's persistence paid off. The Roundtable agreed they could win the House—and, more importantly, they backed it up with cash. On October 5, Gill cut a check for $200,000, and the Colorado Trial Lawyers Association (CTLA) added another $20,000. Three days later, the American Federation of Labor—Congress of Industrial Organizations (AFL-CIO) kicked in $30,000. Less than two weeks later, Polis sent in $49,000, and the next day Alliance for Colorado's Families got checks from the AFL-CIO for $28,952, the Colorado Education Association for $10,000, the CTLA for $2,000, and Gill for $24,500. By the end of the month, Stryker had added $70,000 and the AFL-CIO increased its commitment by another $20,000.

Both the House and Senate were now in play.

The House and Senate 527s were ready to send rafts of direct mail supporting Democratic candidates, but neither was equipped to run the all-important ground game; that would be handled by Coalition for a Better Colorado.

Coalition for a Better Colorado was run by Paul Lhevine, an affable, smart political consultant who had stumbled into Democratic politics accidentally a decade earlier, when he was invited by a friend to volunteer for Governor Roy Romer's reelection campaign. Lhevine was so good at the technical aspects of running campaigns that within a decade he was managing the Denver mayoral campaign of restaurateur, entrepreneur, and eventual gubernatorial candidate John Hickenlooper. (Despite being a political outsider, Hickenlooper won in a landslide.)

Lhevine recalled an early meeting with fellow Roundtable members Michael Huttner and Beth Ganz when the three discussed what they would do with the $1.5 million provided by the Gang of Four. Their first budget imagined a media-driven blitz, but after some discussion with other Roundtable members they decided on a different approach. While spending that kind of money on paid media could make a splash, they opted for the less visible—but far more effective—approach of grassroots canvassing. "In local politics, the key is personal interaction, door-to-door contact," Lhevine said.

Coalition for a Better Colorado hired Burnside and Associates, a Los Angeles–based political consulting firm, to advise on grassroots field operations. The firm, founded by political consultant Sue Burnside, specializes in "using new technology and traditional grassroots tools (phone banking, voter identification, precinct walking, and neighborhood organizing programs) to create highly individualized and individualistic programs for our clients."

After a while, it became clear that Burnside wasn't delivering what Coalition for a Better Colorado needed. Her people didn't know Colorado. Burnside's contract was terminated, and Rutt Bridges volunteered the services of a Bighorn Center for Public Policy staffer, Tyler Chafee, to Coalition for a Better

Colorado. Chafee, Lhevine said, was so good that the team realized they actually didn't need a national political consultant to build a first-rate ground game. They could do it themselves.

Of course, the $1.5 million budget helped. As Lhevine said later, "fund-raising basically consisted of occasional reminders to donors to let them know we needed payment on their pledges." With the money taken care of, Lhevine and Chafee were free to focus on the nuts and bolts of the operation.

Coalition for a Better Colorado set about building a ground operation from scratch, with the first building block being voter data. At its most basic level, this could be gathered using public information: Coalition for a Better Colorado purchased detailed files in targeted legislative districts from county clerks in Adams, Arapahoe, Bent, Boulder, El Paso, Fremont, Gunnison, Jefferson, Lake, Larimer, Mesa, Otero, Pueblo, Rio Blanco, Routt, and Weld counties. This information was supplemented as Election Day neared. For example, voters who requested absentee ballots were tracked so mail could be timed to hit mailboxes close to the same time as ballots. Roundtable groups such as AFL-CIO, Colorado Conservation Voters, CTLA, CEA, and the National Abortion Rights Action League (NARAL) also helped build the database by contributing their own information.

But to gain an edge in November, Coalition for a Better Colorado would need to supplement its baseline public data with details that would allow Roundtable affiliates to contact voters with customized direct mail and phone calls as Election Day approached. The idea was to find out what an individual voter cared about and then explain to that voter why the Democratic candidate would do a better job on that particular issue.

In August and September, Coalition for a Better Colorado began advertising in *The Denver Post*, *Rocky Mountain News*, *Westword*, and *The Onion* for canvassers. These walkers (750 in all), who were paid between $10 and $11.50 per hour, would be given all the work they could handle. From September 3 through October 8, Coalition for a Better Colorado spent $220,000 on canvassing, and in the four-day get-out-the-vote push between October 30 and November 2, an additional $174,000 was paid to walkers. In all, canvassing ended up being one-third of Coalition for a Better Colorado's total budget.

Canvassers were assigned to targeted areas called regions. Each region had a field director who was responsible for building and executing the canvass operation. Canvassers were given Palm Pilots preloaded with voter information software, including "walk lists" and basic data about the voters, such as the voter's name, age, sex, history of voting in primary or general elections, and so on. Some data fields were blank, so it was the canvasser's job to contact the voter, have a conversation, gather the needed information, and enter it into the Palm Pilot. On the spot, canvassers would record information about a voter's thoughts on the upcoming election.

After a canvasser finished for the day, he or she might head out to the back deck of Ten Lakeside

Drive and enjoy some Chinese food from Wok to You while a Coalition for a Better Colorado staff member put the Palm Pilot into a cradle and uploaded the day's data into the master voter file. The information would be integrated with all of the other voter information in the database. Meanwhile, Coalition for a Better Colorado supplemented its canvassing with phone banks, which yielded essentially the same information as the door-to-door walking. This happened time and again from August through October 2004, giving Coalition for a Better Colorado the most complete and sophisticated data file in Colorado.

The Republicans and Karl Rove used similar technology in Ohio and Florida in 2004, but at the time it was practically unheard of in state legislative races anywhere in the country. The Gang of Four's financial resources made it possible.

"The shift in the way we do politics, from the fifties or sixties to the mid-nineties, it was basically the same," said Beth Ganz, who ran NARAL. "And then all of a sudden, the shift in the late nineties and early in this decade, basically the 2000 cycle to now, it's like night and day. Now voter files are online and easily accessible. You can gather information and track voters' interests and the issues they care about. How you communicate with voters, utilizing social media sites, being able to gather information about individual voters versus having to group people into big, broad categories—that's a massive shift in a pretty short period of time."

"The world seems to shift each election cycle

now with new and improved ways to communicate," she said. "There has been so much Internet technology developed over the last decade and increasingly taken advantage of at every level in races across the country. There were more tools in the toolbox in 2004 than there were in 2002, and have been even more [in] each election year since."

The technology had tangible results, allowing Democratic mail and media consultants to develop targeted messages as election season wore on. According to Republican consultant Todd Vitale, who polled legislative races in 2004, "The brilliance on the Democratic side was more micro-tactical than macro-message. Their efforts were well targeted, they had sharp communications, and clearly they had a lot more resources behind them."

Supplementing Coalition for a Better Colorado's paid canvassers was the old-fashioned muscle of organized labor. The state's AFL-CIO president Steve Adams brought labor into the coalition with the other interest groups and the "limousine liberals" (as he called the Gang of Four) and galvanized his members in a way Colorado had never seen. Adams told researchers at Wayne State University that 2,774 activists from 189 locals worked on the campaign, 1,193 of whom were new volunteers. They knocked on 75,356 doors, made 200,000 phone calls, sent out 341,357 pieces of mail, distributed 40,000 work-site flyers and helped raise more money than ever before.

Republican candidates had no idea what was coming their way.

Chapter Seven

"We Didn't Have a Chance":
The Roundtable Unleashes
Hurricane-Force Winds of Change

For twenty-five years, Keith King was the "Waterbed King" of Colorado Springs. After opening and managing a successful Waterbed Palace on the north end of town, King expanded to seventeen other franchises in Colorado, New Mexico, Oklahoma, Tennessee, Texas, and Virginia. He established an advertising company, a manufacturing company, and a financing company to support the core business.

As 2004 began, King was primed to don a different kind of title. Having sold all of his stores two years earlier, King's focus shifted from business to politics. A former school board member and tireless advocate for school choice, he had been elected to the Colorado state House in 1998 and worked his way up the ranks of Republican leadership. As House majority leader, he was primed to become Speaker.

King served with the current Speaker and the first woman to ever hold that post, Lola Spradley, who was term limited at the end of the year. King played the role of majority leader to perfection, running debates smoothly, keeping the legislative calendar orderly, and serving as the prime partisan of his party.

That meant imposing party discipline on members of his own caucus and ensuring Democrats knew their place. Democratic representative Mike Merrifield, a former teacher and foe of King on education issues, recalled King approaching him once as the legislative session began. "How does it feel to know that none of your bills will pass this year?" King asked.

Sitting on top of a 37–28 advantage, House Republicans went into the 2004 election cycle with the goal of targeting incumbent Democrats to expand their majority. Two in particular—Mary Hodge of Brighton and Liane "Buffie" McFadyen of Pueblo—looked vulnerable.

Spradley and King sent out a mailer to the Capitol lobbyists inviting them to a fund-raiser for the House Majority Fund, a Republican 527. On the front, Spradley's and King's faces peered out from behind the window of a speeding freight train above the words "Majority Express." The message to lobbyists was clear: get on board or get run over. The expectation was that they would give significant amounts of cash to the party that had been in control at the state House for all but four years since 1963.

King's ascension was not due to arm twisting or backroom deals, but simple dedication to his caucus. He paid particular attention to his newer members, such as Representative Jim Welker, who had been appointed the year earlier. King sent out a letter to the lobby in November encouraging them to help Welker, and to those who chose not to adhere to the not-so-subtle initial request, he sent a second letter a month later.

"We haven't heard back from you," it read before once again emphasizing the importance of keeping

Welker in the House and encouraging the legal maximum donation of $400 "before the end of the year."

The lobbyists were already a bit chapped, having been informed by Republican leadership that they were encouraged to attend a class on decorum and how to interact with lawmakers. Spradley, King, and Senate president John Andrews thought some of their behavior over the 2003 session was lacking in civility and "strongly" urged attendance at what longtime *Rocky Mountain News* political columnist Peter Blake called "Remedial Lobbying 101."

They packed into the Old Supreme Court Chambers over two separate days to be told that "professionals never outgrow the fundamentals." There was a sign-up sheet, so lobbyists dutifully put pen to paper and kept their tongues firmly planted in their cheeks until they could find a way to escape without being seen. Included among the crowd were a former Speaker of the House, a former US representative, and several former state legislators.

Republicans looked strong heading into the 2004 elections, and the transition from Spradley to King seemed a fait accompli.

"Nobody thought the Democrats had the resources to take the House," said Representative Rob Fairbank, a Republican from a western Denver suburb. "I don't think anybody projected we would lose... [Keith] took an active role in helping candidates after they were nominated, raising money and walking door to door. [He] was running unopposed for Speaker, and everyone assumed he would be the next Speaker."

King's House 527, the House Majority Fund, went into the 2004 elections with almost $470,000, a significant amount compared to past Republican efforts. "That was the first year the 527s were really active," King recalled. "I raised as much as the House leadership in the previous two election cycles combined." "But," King noted in hindsight, "we didn't have a chance against the resources on the other side."

A resource imbalance wasn't King's only problem. As the summer wore on, it was clear that bitterly divisive Republican primaries in two targeted districts would spill over into the general election, endangering seats that should have been safely Republican.

One contest took place in Greeley, where incumbent Tambor Williams, a moderate Republican, had been appointed by Governor Bill Owens to serve as executive director of the Colorado Department of Regulatory Agencies. Owens then appointed Republican Pam Groeger to fill the remaining few months of the term, setting up a primary between Groeger and small-business owner Bob McFadden.

The primary was anything but friendly, with McFadden calling Groeger "extreme" and Groeger characterizing McFadden as soft on issues like abortion. Animosity between the two Republicans culminated in a bizarre episode that August when someone snapped a photograph of McFadden apparently stealing a Groeger campaign sign from what looked like a front yard. The photograph was reproduced on flyers that were then mailed to Republican voters just before the primary election. According to the *Greeley Tribune*, the flyers "accused McFadden of theft" and read, "Can you trust Robert McFadden in your state House?" and "Tell McFadden integrity counts!"

Groeger won by 108 votes, but her victory turned out to be Pyrrhic. The *Tribune* cried foul, reporting that Groeger's husband and campaign workers had been involved in the stunt. "As it turns out," the *Tribune*'s editors wrote, "McFadden was set up. Groeger campaign workers put the sign in his yard and then waited to snap a picture. The same campaign workers were at her house working on the flyers. Groeger's husband, Tony, even told neighbors about the flyers. Yet, Groeger denied knowledge of the flyers when asked by a *Tribune* reporter on election night. She shrugged off the incident by saying, 'It's politics.'"

The *Tribune* called on Groeger to resign the legislative seat she had held for less than a month. "Tell Pam Groeger integrity counts," they wrote. "If the Republican legislator and candidate believes it does, she must immediately resign. She should vacate the state House District 50 seat the governor appointed her to earlier this month and end her candidacy for the office in the November election."

Calling the yard sign incident a dirty trick, the editorial concluded by saying that "if Groeger steps aside by Thursday, the Republican Party can appoint another candidate to run in November. McFadden would be an excellent choice to do that. He lost the primary election by only 108 votes, and this last-minute stunt may have cost him the race."

Groeger vehemently denied knowledge of the trick (the *Tribune* would later report that a district attorney's investigation cleared Groeger and her husband of all criminal charges), and she said she had no intention to step aside. Nor did McFadden rally behind Groeger's general election campaign. The incident fractured Republicans in District 50, pitting McFadden's supporters against Groeger's. Whatever the truth behind the strange story, the well was poisoned. No amount of diplomacy could pull the party back together.

Meanwhile, Democratic candidate and sixty-two-year-old grandfather-of-five Jim Riesberg walked door-to-door, talking about healthcare, education, and the economy, leading a united Democratic Party into the November election. Although Republicans held a six-point generic party identification lead in District 50, the seat was suddenly in doubt.

A similar situation evolved three hundred miles away, in the Western Slope town of Grand Junction. There, a primary was under way to replace moderate term-limited Republican Gayle Berry, who had represented District 55. Forty-nine percent of likely voters identified themselves as Republicans, while only 34 percent called themselves Democrats. George W. Bush led John Kerry by a similar margin, 56–39.

In an ordinary year, this was a district Democrats had no business even considering.

But 2004 was no ordinary year. The Republican

primary between conservative Shari Bjorklund and moderate Steve Erkenbrack broke down along ideological lines, pitting Republicans against one another. After Bjorklund won the primary, many of Erkenbrack's supporters refused to back her, opting instead to help Democrat Bernie Buescher. Buescher took advantage of the schism, counting over two hundred local Republicans among his donors.

"In the Bjorkland race, it was an ideological fight between conservatives and moderates," said Ted Harvey, at the time a Republican member of the House. "When the moderates lost the primary they supported the Democratic candidate rather than their own party's nominee."

Republicans cringed as they watched their party immolate itself in districts 50 and 55. "Republican leaders in those districts came out and endorsed the Democrats and publicly undermined the Republican nominee," said Harvey. "Our nominees were so wounded that even if they had the money, they probably wouldn't be able to win."

Meanwhile, Democrats were busy sharpening a message that would help cut into leads held by Republican candidates in these and several other districts. While King's Republican caucus emphasized its belief in limited government, lower taxes, and property rights, Democrats directed the conversation to other aspects of the GOP program—what Democrats called "God, guns, and gays," a shorthand term for the conservative social agenda.

"I have a note here [in my files]," Alice Madden remembered, "that says, 'In 2004, the Republican majority leader, who was busy counting votes to become Speaker, said the biggest threat to Colorado was gay marriage.'" As the post-9/11 economic environment took its toll on the state budget, Madden found her opportunity.

"There was a sense—and the Democrats very skillfully took advantage of this—that Republicans were focused on the wrong issues while Rome burned," said Alan Philp, a former executive director of the Colorado Republican Party. "This is when the budget was in a mess, and the Republican legislators hadn't really dealt with it."

Madden's campaign theme emerged: Colorado Republicans were beholden to special interests and only cared about pushing an extreme social agenda, not solving problems. "It frankly wasn't all that hard when that's all they were talking about," she said later. On the flip side, she would present Democratic candidates as being focused on the issues people cared about: the budget, healthcare, education, and the environment.

King couldn't doubt the effectiveness of Madden's message, but he didn't find it all that accurate either. "Ramey Johnson and Pam Rhodes were totally different kinds of Republicans, with totally different values," he said, citing two Republican incumbents in 2004, a moderate and a conservative, who were targeted by Democrats. On school choice, for example, Rhodes supported King's philosophy while Johnson sided with the teachers' union against it. "But the Democratic 527s were running exactly the same kinds of ads against both of them. So that tells me that the Democratic campaign had nothing to do with issues, but was about winning at all costs. Regardless of the values of our candidates, the Democrats would smear them."

In August, ten targeted Republican candidates began to feel the first breezes of what would soon become hurricane-force winds of change.

Targeted mail began to hit, and unlike the Democrats' past efforts, it was focused with laserlike precision on local issues. In District 50, for example, they were delighted to exploit the festering wounds of the Republican primary of just a few weeks earlier. The Roundtable's mail vendor, 360jmg, produced an attractive, full-color mailer that read, "An amazing but true tale of dastardly deeds." It went to 9,172 households in District 50. Inside was a poem:

> Bob McFadden and his wife went to pray like
>   they do each and every Sunday.
> But Pam Groeger cares much more about winning
>   than she does about getting caught sinning.
> So while Bob and his wife were at church, Pam's
>   campaign set about to besmirch.

Her campaign put her sign at Bob's house, so
that when he came home with his spouse...

He would take the sign down real quick, unaware
of her dastardly trick.

And that's what sealed Ol' Bob's fate, because
Pam's campaign was hiding in wait.

When he took the sign down from his lawn, they
snapped a photo and then they were gone.

She accused him of removing her signs without
saying it was her grand design.

Pam and her crew distributed a flyer that could
only have come from a liar.

But then the *Greeley Tribune* did get wise to her
tricks and her schemes and her lies.

They exposed her for going over the line and
have called on her to resign.

So please join us as we hold Pam to account
because integrity from candidates should
count.

The strength and effectiveness of the assault caught Republicans completely off guard. "We just assumed they wouldn't have the money to make a hard run at our fairly secure (candidates) in traditionally Republican districts," Harvey said later. "They attacked our incumbents with very focused, very targeted resources and poll-driven messages tailored for each district. We had never seen anything like that in Colorado legislative politics before. Everybody had run on state issues before, but in 2004 the Democrats tailored their message district by district."

Harvey's House colleague Rob Fairbank began to wonder whether his party might actually be on the cusp of losing its majority for the first time in nearly three decades. "Beginning in early fall, polling numbers began to show that some of our members were in trouble," he recalled later.

Meanwhile, the mail kept coming. The pace was relentless. The final month was dizzying. "That was the first year the Gang of Four got involved, and they held back their money until the last four weeks," recalled Harvey.

On the Western Slope, Democrat Kathleen Curry was supported by five pieces of mail to 11,891 households, sixty radio spots over a ten-day period, and automated calls to Republican voters who didn't participate in the primary election. The mail dropped on October 13, 19, 21, 25, and 28 to all active unaffiliated voters and newly registered Democrats since the 2002 election. Including the field campaign, the Roundtable's total spending on the race was estimated to be roughly $75,000.

In the southeastern part of the state, Democrat Wes McKinley received more than $80,000 of support, six mailers to 7,372 households, one radio spot that ran for ten days, and two print ads that ran for two weeks. McKinley's targeted voters included all active, unaffiliated, newly registered Democrats since 2002 and active Republicans under fifty who hadn't recently voted in primaries.

In Arvada, just northwest of Denver, Republican incumbent Representative Bob Briggs was getting pummeled with negative mail.

Everyone at the Capitol loved Briggs, even the Democrats. He didn't fit the stereotype of the Republican legislator the progressive grassroots had grown to dislike, but he had committed the unforgivable sin of living in a competitive district. In 2004, he again faced Democrat Debbie Benefield, whom he had defeated by only 357 votes two years earlier. When Republican leadership polled the race in early August, it showed voters' generic party preference leaning slightly toward Democrats, 45–42. Briggs slightly outperformed his district's partisan dynamics, but still trailed Benefield in a head-to-head matchup, 44–43.

Briggs could have been Mother Teresa, but with numbers like that he was going to be targeted. It would be a close race, and that meant things were about to get nasty.

"I think Bob Briggs is the nicest guy," said Madden later, "but he voted no on this domestic violence bill that was a great bill. He voted no and so the cover of the mailer we sent out had a woman with a black eye. I mean that was pretty intense, obviously."

It was one of more than a dozen targeted mailings that accused him of, among other things, restricting drugs for kids, pregnant women, and seniors in need.

One featured a woman on the phone doing her nails and the words "Bob did what?" next to her astonished face. The other side stated, "That's right...Bob Briggs voted against everything we care about" in large font, and then in smaller print, "He voted against lowering drug costs, against improving public schools, even against unemployment benefits for victims of domestic violence and prenatal care for pregnant mothers."

Opened up, the mailer portrayed Briggs's opponent, Democrat Debbie Benefield, as a "moderate with a commonsense plan for working families." At the top, their names were positioned side by side as "House Candidate Debbie Benefield—Commonsense moderate" and "State Representative Bob Briggs—Shameful extremist."

Sometimes, 360jmg's mail practically screamed for attention. "Who do I see about my prescription drug costs?!" shouted an angry woman wielding a rolling pin, her hair in curlers and her head swollen to twice its normal size. When the piece was flipped over, voters saw that "Bob Briggs is directly responsible for our high drug prices." It was he who voted against lowering the cost of Albuterol, Allegra, Ambien, Celebrex, Fosamax, Lipitor, Prevacid, Zoloft, and a dozen others. "Briggs sold us out to big drug companies," the piece continued. "Big prescription drug companies know who their go-to guy is in Denver—State Representative Bob Briggs."

Despite the unprecedented tsunami of negative mail, Republican leadership at the Capitol refused to believe he was in trouble. "'It's a fairly close district," King told *The Denver Post* that summer. "I think it's a seat we're going to continue to win, and Bob will win because of his experience and the way he represents that district."

But everywhere he went, Briggs saw Coalition for a Better Colorado's paid canvassers. Being the guy he was, he introduced himself, asked questions, and quickly realized he was in a lot of trouble.

"I walked 80 percent of my district in 2004," said the sixty-six-year-old Briggs. "I noticed independent walkers for the Democrats. They all carried PDAs. Each walker was promised that he or she would be given that PDA at the end of the campaign. Each person talked to was recorded in the PDA and that information [was] moved to a main frame in the evening. That information was made available to the next walker so that person would know who had talked to the voter and what was talked about." Those voters would then also receive positive mailers about Benefield, who had once run the county parent-teacher association.

The coordination and effectiveness of the Democratic push was unprecedented. And as the leaves changed from green to brilliant yellows and reds, Briggs began to worry.

Chapter Eight

Circular Firing Squad:
A Story of GOP Fratricide

Golden, Colorado, doesn't feel like a suburb, even though it's just fifteen miles from the skyscrapers of Denver. Just west of Golden's historic downtown, the imposing Rocky Mountains rise at steep angles from the valley bottom. To the east, two flattop mesas bracket the Coors Brewery, founded in 1873 to slake the thirst of miners who flocked to Colorado's mountains in search of gold. The combination of topography and history make Golden feel so isolated that the Golden Economic Development Commission pitches it to nearby Denverites as "Home of the two-hour vacation."

Golden's state representative Ramey Johnson had been first elected to the state House just two years earlier. She worked hard and was well liked by her constituents. But as the 2004 election season wore on, she, like her colleague Bob Briggs to the north, couldn't shake the feeling that she was in trouble.

For one thing, the redistricting bill had become an albatross. "Many of us had reservations about this bill and the manner in which it was introduced. Frankly, we didn't have a choice," she said. "A yes vote was expected at the national level, and strong-arm tactics were used in order to get that yes. After it passed, I knew I/we had a problem." Before the bill, Johnson held joint town hall meetings with the Democrat who represented her area in the Colorado

Senate, Moe Keller. As Johnson later reflected, "the word from the Republican Party was for me to stop joining Senator Keller. Ironically, after the redistricting bill passed, she did not want to be seen with me."

It wasn't just redistricting that worried Johnson. She felt the party had overreached on certain issues, and it hurt candidates in competitive districts like hers. "There was an arrogance on the Republican side of the aisle that eventually took us all down," she said later. "The Republican caucus introduced many bills relating to social issues—some bills were consciously introduced to put other Republicans 'on record.' There was no concern regarding my reelection needs by other members of the caucus or the party."

She voted with the Republican caucus by her estimation "75 to 90 percent of the time." That may not have been enough for some members of her caucus, but it was too much for the Roundtable. Early data showed Johnson leading, but vulnerable. A Republican survey in July showed Johnson leading Democrat Gwyn Green 40–29. The Roundtable's consultants tested the race and found it close too, with Johnson ahead 39–31. With an effective campaign, Johnson could be beaten.

Although internally Roundtable members described Johnson as "a moderate," their eventual strategy would focus on painting her as an extreme conservative. This was necessary, a Roundtable memo noted, because the Democratic challenger, Green, was not "a very strong candidate." "We're going to have to put all the focus on Johnson," they concluded. That meant going negative.

Eight mail pieces were sent out to 10,000 households in Johnson's district to all active unaffiliated voters, newly registered Democrats, and active Republicans under the age of fifty who don't vote in primaries. All contained negative messages. The pieces hit mailboxes on October 7, 14, 18, 19, 21, 25, 27, and 28.

One mailer compared Johnson to a pig.

"Airbrushed lipstick with a tiara—very expensive mailing. I still have it," she said. "It stated on the front, 'No matter how you dress it up, it still stinks.' When you opened it up, there was my picture and selected votes with their 'spin.'"

A caricature of Elvis in a purple suit leapt off another piece, next to the question, "Can you spot an impersonator when you see one?" The other side said, "Ramey Johnson only impersonates someone who cares about you. Her real record is extreme."

Still, she continued going door-to-door, visiting many homes twice during the last couple of months. "I could see I was having problems based on conversations at the door. I instinctively knew the race was tightening up." The constant hammering by Alliance for Colorado's Families was taking its toll. "If people hear the same negative message often enough, they believe it," Johnson learned.

But in a million years, Johnson would never have guessed what happened next.

Eleven days before the election, on a Friday, she received a call from Bob Schaffer, a former US representative (R-CO) and the candidate who had lost to Pete Coors in the Republican US Senate primary three months earlier. He said he needed to meet with her urgently and left two numbers for her to call back.

"I tried unsuccessfully to reach Schaffer at both numbers on Saturday morning and then proceeded to canvass one precinct for the second time," she said. "While walking, I was given a mailing that had hit the door that morning or the previous day from Bob Schaffer...Because the man thought it so vile, he had actually torn it in half."

The mailing, from a 527 Johnson had never heard of, criticized her stand on school vouchers, accusing her of "not listening to parents," caving in to "teachers' union bosses," and "refusing to put children first." "Venomous" was how *The Denver Post*'s Bob Ewegen described the piece.

Johnson was stunned and couldn't fathom why someone with an obviously conservative perspective would attack her on the eve of the general election, especially when the only possible beneficiary would be her liberal opponent. She thought Ronald Reagan's eleventh commandment, "Thou shall not attack fellow Republicans," was being violated, and she couldn't believe her party would let it happen.

She called Republican majority leader Keith King, who encouraged her not to do anything until he made some calls. Four or five days later, King called back and acknowledged the negative mail had come from Schaffer.

"I told [King] then that the letter had thrown the seat. He didn't believe me," she said.

Johnson would go on to lose by forty-eight votes out of more than 27,000 cast.

Chapter Nine

"Financial Atomic Bombs": The Roundtable Turns a Senate Race Inside Out

As he stood with Fort Collins mayor Ray Martinez the Saturday before the election, Governor Bill Owens felt helpless.

They were at the Colorado State University football game, outside Hughes Stadium, shaking hands and greeting fans as they arrived for the Rams' Mountain West Conference showdown with their rival to the south, the University of New Mexico. Martinez was running for the Colorado Senate in District 14 and had his party's most popular figure at his side to demonstrate the importance of the race.

"The Martinez race was the key to the state Senate," Owens said of his friend's candidacy.

The fifty-two-year-old had been comfortably elected mayor of Fort Collins on three separate occasions in nonpartisan races. The district favored Republicans who had a voter registration edge of 38 percent to 31 percent over Democrats, and Martinez's personal history was the kind political consultants dream about.

Given to the state orphanage at eight days old, he was adopted at five by a family in Fort Collins. As a boy he shined shoes, polishing the wing tips of the mayor, the city manager, and other leading community members all the while telling his family, "One of these days, I'm going to wear those shoes."

He served in the US Army and was decorated for his service in Vietnam. Returning to his hometown, he served on the city's police force for twenty-four years and found time to publish two books and write a weekly column for the local paper.

As a Hispanic Republican, he was feted by the party's leaders as an individual who could broaden the party's appeal among crossover voters.

His popularity rating as his city's chief executive regularly hit 70 percent, so it came as no surprise when a baseline poll that summer taken by Republican pollster Vitale & Associates showed Martinez with a comfortable seventeen-point lead, 53 percent to 36 percent, over his Democratic opponent, Representative Bob Bacon.

Bacon's appeal was legitimate as well, having been a public school teacher in the city for thirty-one years, then serving on the school board before moving on to the state House. He was known for his advocacy of kids and public schools in general. It would be a close race between two excellent candidates.

The Roundtable understood the race's importance as well and had targeted the seat as a must-have for Democrats to retake control of the Senate. The Democratic incumbent, Peggy Reeves, was term limited and stepping down, creating a vacancy both parties desperately wanted to fill.

In addition to mail, automated calls, and paid walkers, the Roundtable bought television advertising, both on the Fort Collins cable system and on the Denver network affiliates. Their message boiled down to these four words: "Ray likes to travel." The slogan became the basis for a website (www.raylikestotravel.com) and the theme the Roundtable's 527s hit time and again.

"Ray Martinez likes to travel," the thirty-second spot began. "As mayor, he traveled to places like New Orleans and Key West, enjoying fancy hotels and meals, costing taxpayers $65,000."

"Thanks, Ray," a citizen chimed in.

"Even charging us for his lattes, health spa fees, dry cleaning, minibar drinks, and extra night stays."

"Thanks, Ray," said another voter.

"But Ray bills us even when he's home," the narrator said. "He's reimbursed for the miles he drives to City Hall every single day. Ray Martinez likes to travel, but should we foot the bill?"

"Yeah, thanks, Ray."

Martinez called the tactics dirty politics.

"[The ads are] totally blown out of proportion," he told the *Rocky Mountain Collegian*, a newspaper in town. "There is no truth, no merit to them. Trips that I take, first of all, I'm supposed to sell the city to other cities, other companies, and other organizations to make sure we're on the map in Fort Collins, and we've done it."

"Here's an example. Some of the comments they made were about running up a bar tab, okay, at a bar. If you fly in on a late flight and the restaurant is closed at nine o'clock or ten o'clock, you have to eat at the bar. It's the only place where you can eat."

"The minibar they're talking about—I go out for a jog, I come back in, shower up, and grab a bottle of water or a bottle of orange juice. It's lead to believe that I'm sitting in my room drinking, and that's not the case. The spa that they're talking about is running on a treadmill. Now, a couple of times I admit I think that must have got mis-billed or something because I usually pay for those things...That's what that is. It's not getting a massage and all these things they mislead the reader to believe."

"Yes, the trips are worth [the money spent]. Yes, they're needed. Yes, you bring ideas back that help our city and the people here."

"I have a take-home pay of $660 a month. I think I average about $2.00 an hour from the city of Fort Collins. It's not a bad deal for the people; it's really a good deal. People think I earn $60,000 a year being the mayor. You don't. This is strictly your own energy. So I'm not even making, what do they call it? Minimum wage. I'm barely making that."

When Vitale & Associates went into the field again on September 29 and 30, they found a dramatically changed landscape. Martinez's seventeen-point edge in July had been narrowed to four points, 46–42.

The majority of voters (54 percent) thought the ads were "more about politics than anything else," but Vitale & Associates cautioned Republicans that "this could become a much bigger problem if [the] Dems couple this with another similar hit and target to [independent voters]."

They did. The Roundtable's missives kept coming—on television, on radio, in the mail, on people's phones, and at their front doors. Large numbers of teachers from across the state volunteered to head north to Fort Collins to canvass for Bacon. Critics later argued that coordination between the teachers' unions and the Bacon campaign violated Colorado state law, but a decision by the Colorado Supreme Court eventually cleared him of wrongdoing.

Just when the Roundtable's polling showed they had damaged Martinez, perhaps fatally, the "Thanks, Mr. Bacon" commercial debuted. It showed the retired teacher with kids who said, "Thanks, Mr. Bacon," after an announcer described his efforts to cut bureaucracy on the school board and increase education standards at the Capitol.

Vitale & Associates' last poll was done on October 20 and 21 and Martinez, who was up seventeen points just a few months earlier, was finished. He trailed Bacon by fifteen points, 53–38. "It was a sea change," said former Republican Party executive director Alan Philp. "Ray Martinez was a very good mayor, an honest man, but they found a weakness in him and they drove a stake in his political heart."

Martinez and Owens put on a good face as they campaigned in front of the Colorado State University football stadium. After shaking hands and waving at supporters, they sat together to watch the game, which unfolded in very much the same way Martinez's candidacy had. The Rams opened the game with a strong eighty-yard drive, sending the green and gold faithful into a frenzy on a thirty-seven-yard touchdown pass. Things looked great at halftime, but three turnovers in the second half took their toll and the Rams' lead evaporated. They lost 26–17.

The metaphor was not lost on Owens, who watched as $500,000 was spent by the Roundtable on behalf of Bacon.

"Here we were, standing on street corners the old-fashioned way, while TV advertisements were pounding him on a daily basis," he said. "As we watched the financial atomic bombs dropping around us, we felt helpless. There was nothing we could do to compete with their resources."

"Their dollars moved poll numbers dramatically. Martinez was winning until the crushing preponderance of their activity took its toll."

Part Three
Success

Chapter Ten

Election 2004:
A Great Night for the GOP—
But Not in Colorado

When the polls opened at 7:00 AM on Tuesday, November 2, 2004, Coloradans joined growing lines at schools, fire stations, and churches. Temperatures were among the coldest so far of the season. A hard freeze had taken place overnight and the mercury hovered in the teens in Denver and struggled to reach ten above in many of the mountain communities.

With voter turnout expected to be 70 to 75 percent, many people arrived early, trying to get a jump on their neighbors and avoid the longer lines expected later in the day. Before November 2, 850,000 voters had cast their ballots by mail, a tenfold increase from the 75,000 just four years earlier.

Of the state's roughly 3 million registered voters, more than 1 million were independent, and Republicans outnumbered Democrats by 178,000 voters.

The election would be overseen by Deputy Secretary of State Bill Hobbs and long-serving election officers Bill Compton and Drew Durham. Secretary of State Donetta Davidson had rushed to Arizona the day before to be with her brother, who was in a coma following a motorcycle accident. The governor had a state plane ready to bring her back if the situation was warranted.

But Davidson would not be needed. Small glitches

popped up throughout the day, but nothing dramatic enough to raise the ire of either party or any of the candidates. The forecasted long lines materialized throughout the state, and when polls closed there were still thousands of people waiting to cast their ballots.

At 7:55 PM, the first local results began to trickle in. Early returns showed Pete Coors with a slight lead over Ken Salazar (50 percent to 49 percent) in the US Senate race and President George W. Bush up comfortably over Senator John Kerry (53 percent to 46 percent).

The only commonality between the two major political parties that night in Colorado was that they each chose a Marriott Hotel to celebrate what they hoped would be a historic election.

The Republicans had used the Denver Tech Center Marriott in the last couple of elections. Success breeds superstition. In 2000, the party had captured the presidency. In 2002, Senator Wayne Allard was reelected to a second term over Tom Strickland, Governor Owens won reelection in a landslide, and Bob Beauprez captured the newly created seventh congressional district by a mere 121 votes, the closest congressional race in the country. In 2004, their stage design reflected their confidence with a banner proclaiming "Victory in the Rockies."

The Democrats, meanwhile, were hoping the new City Center Marriott would provide them with new results. Their gathering grew so quickly, fire marshals required the hotel to open up adjoining rooms to its basement banquet room to accommodate the huge crowds. The stage was adorned with a giant sign that read simply "Believe."

The crowds pushed closer to the local television station monitors that were updating numbers as quickly as the Associated Press provided them. By 8:25 PM, the president's lead had grown to 54–45, and Coors maintained his slight lead.

The waiting was, at times, interminable. Political insiders were on the phones with their sources in the field and at the offices of county clerks, trying to tabulate the numbers.

By 8:50, Bush had surged ahead further, both in Colorado and across the country. Coors had fallen slightly behind. Tim Russert described the situation for the presidential race as "the exact replay of 2000," with the keys being Florida and Ohio, and the president continued to lead in each.

The Republican crowd cheered the numbers and Governor Owens did live interviews with some of the local affiliates, telling their reporters that major Republican counties had not yet reported.

"There are lots of votes to be counted for Pete Coors and President Bush," he said. The crowd roared.

The glee inside the central Republican ballroom was not shared by the man who would be Speaker. Republican state House majority leader Keith King, who was upbeat when the evening began, was beginning to comprehend the significance of the results at the bottom of the screen. He would not be Speaker after all.

Even as Owens played the brave general to the cameras, he knew his army was losing the battle for the legislature. "As the results came in," he said, "it was clear they [Democrats] had aggressively and smartly put their financial advantage to work to win the legislature. Race after race, which would typically be 53–47 or 55–45 Republican, became Democratic."

By 9:12, it was clear the Colorado Senate would be controlled by Democrats. Bacon was up 54–42 over Ray Martinez and Democrats had picked up a seat by knocking off suburban Republican incumbent Bruce Cairns, despite his party's predictions all year long that his "strong grassroots organization and tireless energy" would be to his advantage.

Just before 10:00, Bush adviser Karen Hughes predicted victory: "We will win Ohio and Florida and give President Bush four more years." Denver's local NBC affiliate called the state for President Bush.

The Republican crowd went wild.

At Democratic headquarters, one reporter said, "You can't escape the fact there's a palpable disappointment here as the state went to President Bush."

Meanwhile, in the various suites at the respective hotels, candidates and consultants watched a different set of numbers. Coors's staff had seen their candidate consistently poll 3 to 5 percentage points behind the president in Colorado, so the larger the president's margin of victory, the better they liked their chances.

Their polling was off, though. As the president's lead consistently ranged 8 to 9 percent over Kerry, Salazar was slowly increasing his lead over Coors. At 10:10 PM, NBC called the Senate race for Salazar. That same evening, Salazar's brother, John, would win western Colorado's seat in the US House of Representatives, giving both Salazars the distinction of having taken formerly Republican seats in the same year.

By then, Alice Madden and King both knew their fates. One by one, House seats targeted by the Roundtable slid into the Democratic column.

As reality set in, King began calling Republican members who had managed to survive the Roundtable's onslaught to congratulate them on their victories. "And, oh, by the way," he said, "we're no longer in the majority."

Madden, meanwhile, began to cry.

"It's funny because I always knew we could do this, and I always knew if we could actually reach the voter...I just felt like if we can get the message out, because I was so unimpressed with my first four years down there..." she said. "There just wasn't this grand GOP plan being pushed forward. It was just... unimpressive."

Others in her suite were not as convinced coming into Election Night.

"You just don't know," said Jared Polis. "You never know. We didn't really believe it until we saw the results because it was unprecedented. We didn't know it would happen. And yet, it did happen. That was when it sunk in. We were at the hotel, celebrating, and most of the people were sad because Kerry lost and there was this little room where we were all just cheering and thrilled and happy."

"It was a terrific night nationally," said the GOP's Philp. "We picked up a bunch of US Senate seats. George Bush won reelection. And here in Colorado, it was a fairly depressing outcome where we lost a US Senate seat, we lost both houses of the legislature, and we lost the third congressional district as well. I remember running into the governor late that night as he was packing up, and we knew it was going to be a rough ride for his final two years."

It wasn't until 10:30 that the media caught on. Colorado's preeminent independent pollster, Floyd Ciruli, who worked as a political analyst for the NBC affiliate, convinced the station's producers that the results of the down-ballot races were the most surprising story line of the night.

"We do have some news to report about the state legislature," the anchor began. "Democrats have taken control of both chambers."

Incredibly, six of the state House districts won by Democrats that night were also carried by Bush on the same ballot. "This is very big news," Ciruli said, "and it has significant implications for the future of this state."

In the aftermath of the 2004 elections, political observers on both sides of the aisle woke up to the reality that Colorado's political dynamics had changed in a fundamental way. Democrats saw it as a comeuppance for Republicans, who had enjoyed a financial advantage for years and were finding out what it meant to be outspent for once. The *Rocky Mountain News* later reported that Rutt Bridges "makes no apologies for his financial support." "I think Democrats got tired of showing up at a gun fight with a knife," he told the paper.

Governor Owens, who now had to spend his final two years in office dealing with a hostile legislature, saw it differently. "They bought the state. We ought to treat this the way we treat naming rights to football stadiums—let's just put Pat Stryker's and Tim Gill's names on the gold dome of the Colorado state Capitol, because that's what happened." While many factors played a part, Owens pointed to one in particular. "Before campaign finance reform was passed, people tried to use money to influence an individual legislator here or there. Nowadays, big donors just buy them by the dozen."

However one chose to interpret 2004, it was immediately clear that the game had changed. Forever.

Chapter Eleven

Taking It to the States Part One:
Tim Gill Draws GOP Blood in Iowa

Almost seven hundred miles away, Danny Carroll had no reason to worry about what happened in Colorado. It didn't affect him, and besides, he had work to do.

The owner of Carroll's Pumpkin Farm in Grinnell, Iowa, had just won reelection to the Iowa House of Representatives, where he served as the Republican speaker pro tempore. Now it was time to focus on a key piece of his legislative agenda: amending the Iowa Constitution to declare that marriage can only be between one man and one woman.

A strong social conservative, the six-term legislator believed that legal recognition of gay unions posed a direct threat to the family. Although state statutes codified the traditional definition of marriage, the Carroll amendment was intended to prevent judicial activism. "There's one reason to support this constitutional amendment, and that is because [of] what is taking place in the courts in this country," Carroll told the Associated Press. "Yes, we have it on our books, but you and I know in today's society it is easy to go looking for a court somewhere to overturn a law you disagree with."

Most of Carroll's colleagues in the GOP-controlled House agreed with him, but the resolution eventually died in the Senate, where Republicans and Democrats were deadlocked at 25–25.

Some told Carroll he picked the wrong fight and that it could cost him politically. But he didn't back down. His position was a matter of principle, not politics. "Some say that gay issues don't move the numbers in elections so we shouldn't address them," he said later. "But that's not why I ran the resolution— I wasn't thinking about the next election. I did it because it was the right thing to do, period. After the vote, a reporter told me the resolution wouldn't pass the Senate, so why did I do it? I told him, 'Did it ever occur to you that we actually believe in it?'"

Back in Colorado, Tim Gill was paying attention.

Following his home state success in 2004, Gill embarked on an ambitious strategy to change control of legislative chambers in states outside of Colorado. One of those states was Iowa. In November 2006, a tidal wave washed over the state Capitol in Des Moines, giving Democrats a new majority with fifty-four of one hundred House seats and thirty of fifty Senate seats.

One of those Democrats, Eric Palmer, defeated Carroll on his way to the House.

Nobody connected the dots from Colorado to Iowa until a few months later, when Joshua Green of *The Atlantic* reported that Gill had directed checks from around the nation to select candidates for the Iowa legislature.

"Carroll," Green wrote, "was among dozens of targets of a group of rich gay philanthropists who quietly joined forces last year, under the leadership of a reclusive Colorado technology mogul, to counter the tide of antigay politics in America that has generated, among other things, a succession of state ballot initiatives banning gay marriage."

Carroll was flabbergasted when Green showed him the list of out-of-state contributors who helped take him down. "I'll be darned," Carroll told Green. "'That doesn't make any sense.'"

"As we kept scrolling," Green continued, "Carroll began reading aloud with mounting disbelief as the evidence passed before his eyes. 'Denver...Dallas...Los Angeles...Malibu...there's New York again... San Francisco! I can't—I just cannot believe this,' he said finally. 'Who is this guy again?'"

Carroll and five other Iowa Republicans—two in the House and three in the Senate—were just a few of the targets of Gill's nonprofit political organization, the Gill Action Fund. As *Time* magazine later reported, "Recognizing that most antigay initiatives are born at the state level, Gill has developed a national political strategy based on successes in Colorado."

Iowa was but one part of a national strategy. After a careful process of selecting state legislative races around the country where a concentrated amount of money could tip the balance of political power, Gill notified members of his donor network. They, in turn, sent maximum direct contributions to seventy candidates in at least fifteen states. In addition to the six legislative races in Iowa, records from the nonpartisan National Institute on Money in State

Politics indicate that Gill targeted nine seats in Colorado, two in Maryland, three in Massachusetts, eight in Michigan, six in Minnesota, two in Montana, three in Ohio, five in Oklahoma, five in Oregon, three in Pennsylvania, and six in Washington.

Given the close nature of those races, Gill's precisely targeted selection directly aided in the election of more than fifty Democratic state legislators nationwide. Even more importantly, Gill was a key factor in Democratic takeovers in the House and Senate in Iowa as well as the state Houses in Michigan and Oregon.

"They've taken an in-state model and applied it to the entire country," *Time* quoted Denver political analyst Floyd Ciruli as saying. "Gill [and his people are] incredibly strategic. They simply don't waste money. They put their funding where they can take control of legislatures."

"I'm not sure that everyone really understands how potent [Gill] is, but he now has to be the number-one gay rights advocate in the country in terms of funding and strategy," Ciruli told *Time*. "They're taking significant contributions and putting them brilliantly in legislative environments where a few seats changing will change the entire control of a state."

The focus on local races instead of higher profile contests was consistent with the strategic decision made by the Roundtable in 2004. In a speech at the Democratic National Committee in 2008, Gill explained to a group of gay activists why they should lower their sights if they wanted to achieve greater changes in public policy. "Every single advancement in gay rights has been made at the state level," he told the crowd. "There is no example of something that was done at the federal level and then the states went, 'Gosh! We should've done that!'"

"So the most important thing I'm going to tell you that you can do is not what you're doing here [at the Democratic National Convention] this week. This week is fun, it's important. But the very most important thing you can do is go back and support those pro-gay state legislators. Eliminate the antigay state legislators."

To those who would criticize Gill for ignoring the power of Congress, he cited Marilyn Musgrave, a then sitting US representative from Colorado who sponsored the Federal Marriage Amendment, which would have codified a ban on gay marriage in the US Constitution. By shaping state legislatures, he argued, he could change the composition of future Congresses—at a fraction of the cost.

"Marilyn Musgrave started on the school board," Gill told Robert Frank, author of *Richistan: A Journey through the American Wealth Boom and the Lives of the New Rich*. "She would have been much cheaper to nuke when she was on the school board or even when she was in the legislature. We need to be vigilant and find politicians who are bad and stop them when it's cheap rather than allowing them to get into an expensive position."

Carroll fit the profile perfectly. And although Gill knew about Carroll, Carroll didn't know about

Gill until it was too late. "I'm rather embarrassed to admit that prior to December 2006 I didn't know who Tim Gill, Pat Stryker, and these other out-of-state donors were," he said later. But after reflection, he now knows why they went after him. "They targeted me for four reasons. First, I was in a legislative district they could win. My district includes Grinnell College, a very liberal campus. [Second,] I was the House floor manager of a resolution that would amend the Iowa Constitution to define marriage as between one man and one woman. Third, I was speaker pro tem[pore] of the House, so I was in Republican leadership. And, finally, I was in a state where they could flip both chambers of the legislature to Democratic control. So I had every target on me."

Following Gill's victories in 2006, conservative groups sounded a national alarm about the reclusive multimillionaire. In 2008, Focus on the Family's *Citizen* magazine featured a profile on him, calling him "perhaps the most powerful force for homosexual activism in American politics."

"Dozens of conservative politicians have found themselves in Gill's crosshairs—and out of office as a result," the article reported. "Political veterans are marveling at his impact."

Focus on the Family was most interested in the same subject that held Gill's attention: concrete changes in social policy, particularly related to legal recognition of gay unions. "New Democrat majorities in New Hampshire promptly passed a civil-unions law. In Iowa, where Carroll lost his seat and the Republicans lost the House, the Democrat legislature enacted a homosexual nondiscrimination law. And Oregon's new Democrat lawmakers pushed through variations of the aforementioned laws."

In Colorado, where Gill started, Republican state senator Josh Penry told *Citizen* that the new Democratic agenda was "windmills, mill levies, and a million paybacks to Tim Gill." Among the paybacks listed were a gay adoption bill, a nondiscrimination statute, and a law changing the definition of what constitutes a "family" for state law purposes.

On the other side, gay publications praised Gill for his work in "chamber management"—a shorthand term to describe the targeting of state legislative races to achieve gay-friendly majorities. Writing in *The Advocate*, the nation's most prominent gay newsmagazine, Kerry Eleveld described the Gill Action Fund's work as "developing a hit list of the community's worst enemies, identifying our best friends, and doing whatever has to be done to get the next hate-crimes bill passed or constitutional amendment killed at the state level."

Eleveld was particularly interested in Gill's ability to attract large donors and sell them on his state-based vision. "After attending the first conference where Gill Action rolled out its path to equality to about 300 potential donors in the spring of 2006, a lightbulb went off" for an anonymous donor interviewed by Eleveld. "I was thinking, Thank God, this is the first time that I've had a sense that maybe the political dollars that I'm giving are going to make a strategic difference," said the donor. In 2006, the donor "invested" almost $50,000 in state races in eleven states, writing direct checks to candidates identified by Gill. "You can make a difference with $500 in some races," the donor said. That was a contrast to giving in higher profile races, where the donor had focused his contributions before buying into Gill's approach. "Even if you gave the max to a Senate or a House candidate at the federal level, you don't even move the needle."

In 2008 Carroll tried, unsuccessfully, to recapture his seat. Again, he lost. And again, his opponent enjoyed the support of out-of-state gay donors coordinated by Gill. Reflecting on Gill's influence, Carroll is of two minds. "On the one hand, I don't like outside money influencing local races," he said. "Tim Gill doesn't care about what happens in Iowa, he's just interested in promoting homosexuality. I understand that. On the other hand, when I ran again in 2008, people knew that my opponent was financed by homosexual activists, but they voted for Palmer anyway. So if it doesn't bother them, that's the way it is. It's a little bit depressing that homosexual activists have that much clout to manipulate local elections. Why are people so asleep that they can be influenced that way?"

For Gill's part, influence is the name of the game. "Progress for equality will continue state by state, law by law," Gill wrote in the Gill Foundation's 2008 annual report. "Warren Buffett is fond of saying that when others are bold, be timid," Gill continued. "And when others are timid, be bold. So that we can address the needs and take advantage of the opportunities that lie before us, I've decided to be bold."

It remains an open question whether Carroll would have won had he not chosen to run a resolution banning gay marriage. But to him, it doesn't matter. "Two thousand six was my seventh campaign for the Iowa House," he said later. "The Democrats were after me every year. They were always trying to defeat me. I may have lost in 2006 anyway, but even if my position on the constitutional amendment cost me the race, I would absolutely do the same thing again."

When asked why, Carroll doesn't hesitate. "Because I believe in it," he says with resolve. "And those are my values."

Chapter Twelve

Elevating the Game:
The Roundtable Becomes CoDA

Bill Menezes didn't like what journalism had become. So the former reporter left his stable job at the public relations agency, where he loved his colleagues, his clients, and his quality of life, to fight for its soul.

"I grew up in old-school news journalism, from college through the first nine years of my career at the AP [Associated Press] and beyond, where accuracy was paramount and the consequences for poor fact-checking were severe," he said. "We're now in an age where virtually no local newspaper or television station has an ombudsman or reader/viewer advocate on staff, and where some editors vigorously criticize the pointing out of repeated factual inaccuracies in their product as nitpicking."

So, in 2006, when he was approached to serve as editorial director for a website called Colorado Media Matters, an offshoot of the Washington, DC–based Media Matters for America, a progressive nonprofit whose goal was to "correct conservative misinformation" in the media, it seemed the logical fit.

"We're in an age where the public typecasts media so strongly that people are unaware how some-times-shoddy journalism at a 'liberal' news outlet such as Colorado Public Radio sometimes has helped to stealthily, if unintentionally, promote conservative political messages," he said. "The progressive aspect of it was never as important to me—I remember during the interview process asking whether it mattered that I had no real pedigree in progressive politics; it didn't—as the media element. It was merely serendipitous that there was a progressive group doing such work in Colorado and that there was ample material to work with in terms of conservative misinformation in the media."

Menezes, a devout fan of *Jeopardy!* and onetime contestant, brought what one of his previous editors described as "fantastic research skills" to the table. Media Matters paid him a six-figure salary to ensure that political reporters and editors throughout Colorado did their jobs accurately, and when they didn't, to call them on it publicly.

By the time Media Matters branched out to Colorado in the summer of 2006, it had posted roughly five thousand examples of "fact-based research and activism [that] has held the media accountable [and] instilled higher standards." Typically, that meant criticizing the mainstream media for being too easy on Republicans.

With a staff of twelve and backing from the Gill Foundation and other progressive donors, Menezes set out "to challenge local media every day to do their best to serve the citizens of your state. And when they don't, we ask you to join with us in letting them know it."

The mainstream media was too conservative for Menezes, and Media Matters was the remedy. By putting pressure on television, radio, and print outlets,

Media Matters existed to expose right-wing bias, especially on talk radio.

"They have the megaphone," he said. "The reality is, the commentary media in Colorado is overwhelmingly dominated by conservative voices, but it served to their detriment. The fact they were so loud highlighted certain elements of their base. It's kind of like being upside down on a house you didn't pay anything to buy. When the going's good, it's great. But when you're down, you're screwed, and in terms of messaging, they were screwed."

Menezes and Colorado Media Matters were just one small part of the growing network that looked and acted completely different than the Roundtable of two years earlier. In 2004, the Roundtable's operations were limited to a handful of 527s focused on winning the state legislature. Members of the group now aspired to build a permanent, far-reaching progressive infrastructure that would exist year-round, not just during election cycles. The objective was to change Colorado's political landscape completely and permanently.

To accomplish this, members of the Roundtable knew that to meet the challenge the organization would need to grow, both by increasing its donor base and by diversifying the number and kind of nonprofits that comprised the tools in its toolbox. It could no longer simply be focused on elections and voters because other progressive causes needed help no matter what the calendar said.

In January 2005, Tim Gill, Pat Strkyer, Jared Polis, Rutt Bridges, Ted Trimpa, and Al Yates gathered to focus on their new mission. Bridges hosted the meeting at his downtown Denver loft.

For five hours, Colorado's political elite lunched, laughed, and labored to answer some fundamental questions, such as, did it make sense for them to stay together? Did they still have shared and unrealized goals? How tight were their bonds?

Having answered all of these questions in the affirmative, they decided to meet later in the spring to put some detail into their next steps. Two thousand four was merely prologue. If they kept working together, the sky was the limit.

Ever the professor, Yates meticulously developed a formula that would solidify the donor alliance, maintain the coordination among like-minded groups, exploit the weaknesses of conservative candidates, and nurture a favorable electoral environment for candidates who would implement the group's progressive policy goals.

He envisioned three independent strategies that would work together to accomplish these ends. The first focused on collaboration between donors, progressive organizations, and elected officials. The second defined and developed a lasting progressive infrastructure in Colorado. And the third created a network of donors to provide the lifeblood of money into these efforts.

He called his idea the Colorado Alliance.

Unfortunately, it turned out that some Republicans already had a small donor committee called the Colorado Alliance.

And so the Colorado Democracy Alliance (CoDA) was born.

According to internal documents obtained by the conservative news organization Face the State (and later reported by *The Denver Post*), CoDA describes itself to prospective members as "an active collaboration of donors and progressive organizations aligned to build and fund a permanent progressive infrastructure. Its mission is to create a sustainable progressive majority and a progressive Colorado." In particular, CoDA would focus its energy on developing "enhanced, integrated capacities in four key areas: civic engagement and voter mobilization; intellectual content and messaging; leadership development; and media and communications."

Despite the breadth of CoDA's mission, it is not itself a large organization. Its initial 2006 budget was less than $200,000, beginning with two start-up loans each of $38,000 from Stryker and Gill. The organization maintains a small staff that essentially functions as a dating service to match big progressive donors and progressive nonprofits.

Unlike traditional political networks, where parties, candidates, or even vendors determine spending, CoDA's model is totally donor driven. The organization does not give money directly to nonprofits, nor does it act as a financial clearinghouse for contributions.

Instead, it provides a forum where donors gather at a table to meet with nonprofits seeking money.

The Colorado Democracy Alliance has been likened to a political venture capital fund, and the analogy fits well. After evaluating the relative strengths and weaknesses of various nonprofits and taking into account CoDA's broader objectives, at the end of the process the board votes and the staff produces a list of funding recommendations to be circulated to the donors. At that point, donors make direct contributions to the newly selected members of the CoDA network.

CoDA's first meeting took place in January 2006. Donors and their representatives were in attendance, as was Democratic attorney Mark Grueskin. With Grueskin's guidance, the group opted to structure itself as a taxable nonprofit organization, which means it's not required to file reports with the Internal Revenue Service (as it would if it elected to be a 501 or 527 organization). This, combined with the fact that donors directly fund network organizations, makes it extremely difficult to tie CoDA affiliates with their financial backers. In the case of the 501(c)(3) charitable organizations in the CoDA network, which are not required to disclose their donors, it is impossible.

Organizational decisions are made by a board of directors (which includes original Roundtable members Bridges, Gill, and Stryker) in consultation with the general membership. Membership is divided into three tiers: tier one members participate in the decision-making process and are expected to make an annual commitment of $100,000 or more directly to CoDA-identified groups; tier two members commit to a minimum of $25,000; and institutional members (usually business or labor organizations) commit in excess of $400,000.

By 2006, CoDA had added more donors to its ranks, including backers like oil and gas heir Tom Congdon, vacuum cleaner heir Bruce Oreck, and Boulder philanthropist Linda Shoemaker. It added the powerful Service Employees International Union to its list of institutional members, joining the Colorado Education Association, the American Federation of Labor—Congress of Industrial Organizations, and the Colorado Trial Lawyers Association.

CoDA was the Roundtable on steroids: more donors, more money, more nonprofits in the network—and more capacity to shape Colorado's political landscape.

CoDA served as a financial lifeline to groups like Colorado Media Matters. The umbrella of outlets seeking to work toward "progressive" causes grew significantly from 2004, and numerous nonprofits found a new donor base willing to fund their projects.

CoDA documents published by *The Denver Post* showed that dozens of groups interacted with the alliance in one way or another. These groups were established throughout the state and impacted hundreds of thousands of citizens through their work.

For example, CoDA reached out to nonprofits within the minority communities. In the Hispanic community, it funded the Latina Initiative, which seeks to "cultivate, support, and maintain the civic involvement of Latinas in Colorado," and Mi Familia Vota, which helps immigrants become citizens.

CoDA also sponsored the African American Voter Registration and Information Project, which developed the largest database in the state of African American voters.

The organization cultivated an ideas factory in The Bell Policy Center, which described itself as a think tank with a progressive vision. "The Bell" also provides resources for candidates seeking to advocate progressive causes.

The Center for Progressive Leadership was created because "progressive leaders from around the country...saw crucial gaps in training, mentorship, coaching, and support for progressive campaign, organization, community, policy, and political leaders."

Another group, Progressive Majority, set up shop in Colorado "to bring true progressives into politics and create positive change that would last. We're recruiting progressive leaders to run for office who can also galvanize progressive voters who have been shut down by the loud voices of the ultraconservative right."

Of course, the issues important to progressive voters and the nonprofits that promoted them were funded as well. Groups such as Colorado Conservation Voters, Common Cause, the National Abortion Rights Action League, and Planned Parenthood were arguably the largest entities to receive support from CoDA and offered potentially the largest databases of donors and voters in return.

A burgeoning network of grassroots and new media outlets also sought assistance from CoDA. Groups like ProgressNow, created in 2003, became a megaphone for grassroots motivation, fund-raising, and outrage. In time, ProgressNow would have a major impact on the political landscape.

Colorado Ethics Watch, which sought to use "high-impact legal actions" to hold political officials accountable for "unethical activities," often through lawsuits and press releases, received money from CoDA. So, too, did *The Colorado Independent* (formerly *Colorado Confidential*), an online news daily that mixed blogging and traditional journalism.

"CoDA works with all these organizations to foster interaction, to make sure that they have not only the financial resources, but also access to best practices and to the information they need to do their work better," said former CoDA executive director Laurie Hirschfeld Zeller at a presentation to national Democrats in 2008. "We are structured as a taxable nonprofit corporation, but we function as a membership organization. We're working to build a donor community here. We're working to enable their communications with organizations and with political entities, and we do so in a structure that provides privacy for members, but also offers us the flexibility to work in relationships with other political entities that gives us some agility and effectiveness."

CoDA's reach was statewide. Donors helped advocate progressive causes throughout Colorado, and while there was no de facto edict to support certain candidates, its focus on progressive policies made Democrats the inevitable beneficiaries of CoDA's efforts.

"As an outsider looking at it, I've always been impressed with how commonsense and logical it is," said Menezes of his first political job. "It's not complicated. The simplicity's always impressed me. There's an overarching idea that's getting everybody to push in the same direction.

"[CoDA] matched people up with like-minded others. It's basically a facilitator. It's not setting any agenda. When we wondered, how will we find more money to keep our organization going, we turned to CoDA. We were at the receiving and requesting end of the pipeline. CoDA helped get us acquainted with actual donors," Menezes added. And when Colorado Media Matters closed its doors in 2009, it had fulfilled its purpose, having played a key role in tilting the Colorado political landscape in favor of progressive candidates in the 2006 and 2008 election cycles.

Zeller describes CoDA as an "irrigation system," delivering life-sustaining support to dozens of organizations like Colorado Media Matters, each filling a unique space in CoDA's broader electoral agenda. "We provide services to our members in terms of research, advice on their giving, activating their collective interaction, to help make the progressive sector stronger," she said.

"But our role is really to harness the financial resources as well as the brains and the energy of the progressive sector."

Chapter Thirteen

The Trailhead Group: Colorado Republicans Fight Back —And Get Sued

For Colorado legislative Democrats, the 2006 election cycle began just days after the celebration in 2004 ended. Not content to rest on their laurels, they aimed to expand their House and Senate majorities while at the same time protecting their newly elected legislative members from a certain Republican counterassault in 2006.

Just six weeks after Election Day 2004, newly minted Speaker of the House Andrew Romanoff and majority leader Alice Madden were at work on an incumbent protection plan that went well beyond the typical activity of ramping up campaigns during election years. With a vast reservoir of financial resources, they had the luxury of turning the election cycle into a twenty-four-month affair.

The plan committed over $1 million to protecting ten vulnerable incumbents with newsletters, postcards, automated calls, and newspaper ads. By the time 2006 rolled around, this work would shore up any potential weaknesses, making it all the more difficult for Republicans to win back those seats.

In addition to keeping the legislature firmly in their hands, Democrats had another goal: to put a Democrat in the governor's mansion. Republican governor Bill Owens was retiring due to term limits, and the open seat presented a perfect opportunity to complete the trifecta.

Taking on the governor's race would stretch resources, but the Colorado Democracy Alliance (CoDA) was there to fill the vacuum. The Roundtable's principal tools in 2004 had been separate 527s for both the House and Senate, as well as a joint field operation. These would remain in place, albeit under different names, in 2006. The House 527 changed its name from Alliance for Colorado's Families to Main Street Colorado and, according to CoDA's documents, its budget would be $2.85 million. The Senate 527, with an initial budget of $2.65 million, changed from Forward Colorado to Moving Colorado Forward. The legislative field operation changed from Coalition for a Better Colorado to Citizens for Colorado, and it began with a budget of $1.715 million.

In addition to shoring up the 527 capacity that had existed in 2004, CoDA added several new 527s to support its gubernatorial efforts. These were Clear Peak Colorado (described as a war room, with an initial budget of $400,000), Colorado Voter Project (the gubernatorial field operation, with an initial budget of $1.025 million), New West Fellowship (a 527 to attack the Republican gubernatorial candidate, with an initial budget of $1.9 million), and Rocky Mountain Horizons (a 527 to support the Democratic gubernatorial candidate, with an initial budget of $397,500). Along with some money to fund an opposition research arm, the grand total of CoDA's initial budget for 2006 was $11.297 million.

For their part, GOP donors and operatives resolved to fight back. Stung by their 2004 setbacks, Republicans planned to win back the legislature. "I'm optimistic Republicans will take back the House," Alan Philp, former executive director of the Colorado Republican Party, told the *Rocky Mountain News*. "In the Senate, there are too many variables to predict what's going to happen," he said. "But we're going to pick up seats in the House. The question is just how many."

Philp's confidence wasn't unfounded. After all, President George W. Bush had carried the state, and Republicans still enjoyed a significant voter registration advantage, with roughly 1.04 million Republicans to 871,000 Democrats.

More importantly, the element of surprise was gone: Democrats weren't going to catch Republicans flat-footed in 2006. With solid candidate recruitment and better messaging, there was no reason the GOP couldn't reverse the setbacks of 2004. Six of the state House seats held by Democrats had also been won by Bush, creating an instant target list for 2006.

Early in 2005, former Colorado Republican Party chairman (and current University of Colorado president) Bruce Benson approached Philp about heading a new 527 to counter the Roundtable. "Republicans, who have been wide awake since that 2004 shocker, have beefed up their efforts, including forming a new '527 committee,' the Trailhead Group, headed by Philp," the *Rocky Mountain News* reported.

Like a prizefighter who had been stunned by an unexpected blow, the Colorado GOP was rising from the mat to get back in the fight.

Trailhead had the support of key Republican leaders like Governor Owens, former US Senate candidate Pete Coors, and a list of longtime GOP funders. "At the donor level, there was a sense among a few [of] 'let's take it to them and make a point that if they're going to spend millions we're going to spend millions in response,'" Philp said.

According to the Center for Responsive Politics, by the end of the cycle Trailhead would go on to raise over $5.3 million. "There was an effort to try and counter what had happened in 2004 with the creation of not only the Trailhead Group, but some other 527s [in] the Senate and the House, All Children Matter [another 527] and some others," Philp said. "So there was an effort to professionalize our operation more, there was an effort to fund it more, fight back, and recruit better candidates."

The GOP appeared to have a strong gubernatorial candidate in Republican US representative Bob Beauprez. "I went into that election thinking I would win," said Beauprez, a proven vote-getter who had twice won a competitive congressional district in the suburbs of Denver. "Who wouldn't? And I had convinced myself there just wasn't any way that a state like Colorado would elect somebody as inexperienced and I thought as liberal as we would expose [Democratic gubernatorial candidate] Bill Ritter to be."

Ritter, a former Denver district attorney, was the

presumptive Democratic nominee, even though he's a pro-life Catholic. "It's funny because [Republicans] are trying now to look at our playbook and say what pages can we borrow out of that to shift the landscape again," said Ritter. "I was a pro-life Democrat running in a governor's election, and it might have been different if I was running in a US Senate election, but I still had a bevy of people I trust saying, 'You can't win a primary.'"

But, amazingly, the pro-life former prosecutor didn't draw a challenge within his own party.

"That is maybe the single best indication of how Democrats in this state are at a place where they figured, we as a party, need to really live up to this slogan we have about being a big tent party. Republicans say that as well, but we really believe in it," said Ritter. "We really believe it."

Beauprez, on the other hand, found himself in a primary against Marc Holtzman, an independently wealthy political activist who served on Governor Owens's cabinet. While Holtzman was never a threat to win, he did tremendous damage to Beauprez, accusing him of being wishy-washy on a statewide referendum to allow government to keep more tax revenue. Then, when Beauprez reversed his position on a proposal that would make it easier for citizens to initiate ballot measures, Holtzman played gotcha once more. The Holtzman team came up with a label for Beauprez: "Both Ways Bob."

CoDA was taking notes. After Beauprez beat Holtzman at the state Republican assembly, a *Rocky*

Mountain News article foreshadowed Beauprez's political lot with a first line that read, "Republican Marc Holtzman is gone from the governor's race, but he leaves behind a catchy legacy voters can expect to hear more of as the November election looms."

ProgressNow Action, the political 501(c)(4) arm of original Roundtable member Michael Huttner's group ProgressNow, launched a website called www .bothwaysbob.com and created Internet ads citing Beauprez's "both ways" label on issues such as ethics, water, spending, business, and healthcare. Anyone who sent the group a $10 donation received a pair of flip-flops with the phrase "Both Ways" written on them and a photo of Beauprez to boot. Denver's alternative weekly newspaper *Westword* described them as "proof once again that only a hypocritical stance and one false letter separate scandals from sandals."

Another 527 called Citizens for Progress (based out of Washington, DC, and supported by the Democratic Governors Association, the Gill Foundation, the Colorado Education Association, and several labor unions) carried on the theme for nearly three straight weeks on television in Colorado. A pair of fifteen-second ads would bookend at least one commercial break in each newscast from morning until night on Denver's leading stations.

"In Colorado," the commercial's announcer said right after the news anchor had announced they would be right back, "Bob Beauprez said he's for healthcare. But in Washington, Congressman Beauprez sided with the insurance companies to allow them to stop covering women with breast cancer. No wonder they call him 'Both Ways Bob.'"

After commercials from a car dealer, airline, hospital, and local lawyer, the last fifteen seconds before the anchor came back on camera started with, "In Colorado, Bob Beauprez says he's for seniors. But in Washington, Congressman Beauprez voted to make seniors pay more for their healthcare and denied nursing-home care to seniors. No wonder they call him 'Both Ways Bob.'"

The label, coined by a fellow Republican, became a devastatingly effective weapon against Beauprez.

"Right through Election Day, we felt we were forever playing defense," Beauprez said later. "It was pretty obvious that somebody somehow was making sure this was working as a well-oiled machine."

Beauprez didn't help himself. Colorado Media Matters tape-recorded him saying on Colorado Public Radio that "70 percent of African American pregnancies ended in abortion." He later apologized.

To make matters worse, Trailhead—which was supposed to provide air cover for Beauprez—was experiencing setbacks of its own. As the election approached, Philp had to deal with a problem even more irksome than lackluster polling numbers for his gubernatorial candidate: lawsuits.

"[The lawsuits] were designed to be a major distraction and to scare us off from some of the things we were trying to do," Philp said. "The criminal complaints were thrown around with reckless abandon. Any time we'd put up an ad, if they [Democrats] could find anything to latch on to, they'd file a criminal complaint with the district attorney."

And then came the civil suits, courtesy of Democratic lawyers Mark Grueskin and Ed Ramey. "They'd get us in for depositions, try and find out as much as they could about how we operated. There was one week in September of 2006—I remember it. Every day that week I'd get a subpoena or a lawsuit put on my desk." There were so many actions, Philp lost track.

The legal attacks took their toll on donors too. "People who donate to political organizations don't like that fear of uncertainty or being part of a deposition or discovery."

For donors, lawsuits weren't even the worst of it. "A couple of our major donors would get calls in the middle of the night left on their personal business or home voice mails filled with four-letter words accusing them of reprehensible conduct because they had written a check to Trailhead," Philp recalled.

The pace of the lawsuits was dizzying enough to make Trailhead a major story of the election cycle. With all the negative press, Trailhead's ads attacking Democrats were as likely to raise questions about Trailhead as they were to land a blow on the intended target.

Trailhead was dying a death of a thousand cuts, even as CoDA's many organizations, which collectively dwarfed Trailhead, quietly rolled along. One reason for Trailhead's woes was the way it was structured as a single entity, with all of its eggs in one legal basket. As a stand-alone 527, its entire roster of donors could be found in the same set of IRS disclosure forms, making it easy for journalists and political opponents to dissect Trailhead. The same transparency made Trailhead an especially inviting target for lawyers, who only needed to name one defendant and the entire GOP operation would grind to a halt. "One of the lessons of 2006 was that we made a centralized bull's-eye on Trailhead," Philp said later.

CoDA, on the other hand, wasn't one entity, but a loosely related network of dozens of different entities. Each organization was separately governed and filed its disclosure forms (if at all) independently and on separate IRS forms. The effect was to slow down any would-be sleuth who tried to piece together the size and scope of CoDA's operations or the level of its donors' involvement. (As easy as it was for reporters to get their arms around Trailhead, they never fully figured out CoDA until nearly *two years* after the 2006 election cycle was over.)

There was also a tactical advantage to CoDA's decentralized structure. Unlike Trailhead, which could be brought to a halt by a single mistake, CoDA insulated itself against the inevitable missteps that cause problems during campaigns. If one entity struggled or became discredited (as was Clear Peak Colorado when Comcast pulled its advertisements that falsely characterized the voting record of GOP Colorado Senate candidate Matt Knoedler), the other entities kept right on going.

As election season heated up, so did Trailhead's problems. While the lawyers bored into Philp, elements of the CoDA network took to the stage in a balletic display of precisely choreographed coordination.

In mid-September, CoDA affiliate *Colorado Confidential* ran a story questioning the legality of Trailhead's funding. The *Rocky Mountain News* picked up the story, reporting online that "the blog *Colorado Confidential* last week accused the influential GOP group of money laundering, saying donations and contributions to and from other GOP groups don't add up. In turn, complaints were filed with the IRS by [CoDA affiliate] Colorado Citizens for Ethics in Government and with the secretary of state by the Democratic political group [and CoDA affiliate] Colorado Clear Peak."

Shortly afterward, Colorado Media Matters, itself a CoDA affiliate, which had been hammering both newspapers all year for being too soft on Trailhead, complained that "as of September 21, *The Denver Post* had yet to publish a story about recent complaints filed against the Republican-backed Trailhead Group in response to the group's reported financial transactions, despite the *Rocky Mountain News*'s coverage of those complaints."

In the end, Philp saw the lawsuits as having nothing to do with lawyers seeking justice and everything to do with campaign tactics. "Every single lawsuit that was filed against me or against Trailhead was defeated, dismissed, or withdrawn. These were designed to intimidate, they were designed to distract, and to assassinate character. That's what they were about."

Chapter Fourteen

Election 2006:
CoDA Extends Its Lead

Matt Knoedler, an up-and-coming state representative from suburban Denver, was the GOP's best hope to take control of the Colorado Senate in 2006. To get there, he would have to unseat Betty Boyd, the incumbent Democratic senator in District 21.

It would be a hard-fought, expensive race.

Prior to running for the state House in 2004, the thirty-year-old Knoedler advised US representative Tom Tancredo (R-CO) and Governor Bill Owens on energy and natural resources issues. Friends and foes alike knew that Knoedler, who had been called one of the "rock stars" of the Colorado GOP by the *Rocky Mountain News*, was smart and pragmatic. His opponent, Boyd, had recently been appointed to fill the seat after the Democratic incumbent was forced to resign for attempting to use the power of her office to solicit a campaign contribution. The GOP recruited Knoedler to challenge Boyd in what was effectively an open seat.

With control of the state Senate again at stake, Knoedler found himself opposing not just the former nurse and nonprofit manager, but hundreds of thousands of dollars in Colorado Democracy Alliance (CoDA) money.

Knoedler knew the drill. In 2004, the Roundtable targeted eight House Republicans and defeated seven; Knoedler was the only one they couldn't take out. Later, he recalled that being targeted by so much money made him feel "like a bug under a magnifying glass." But he hung on to survive the onslaught of paid door-knockers and, of course, the omnipresent glossy mailers.

Although Knoedler knew what to expect, nothing prepared him for CoDA, the new and improved version of 2004's Roundtable.

Knoedler's parents, who had recently returned from the Peace Corps in Panama, were living with their son when what he describes as the worst of mail began to arrive. "My mom, a lifelong Democrat, former treasurer of the Boulder Democratic Party, opens the mail and there was a piece that said, 'Every parent's worst nightmare,'" he remembered later. "My mom was just in tears."

"Do we need more lobbyists?" asked the mailer. Next to a photo of a smarmy-looking youngster with a briefcase, the piece informed voters that "Matt Knoedler Is Every Parent's Worst Nightmare—Opposing Quality Health Care for Our Kids...It's something you'd expect from a lobbyist. Matt Knoedler cares more about taking care of lobbyist cronies than protecting our kids."

"The crazy thing is," Knoedler said later, "I went to my law firm because it didn't have any state House lobbyists. I didn't want there to be any conflicts of interest. What little lobbying I did was at the federal level."

Knoedler wasn't naive. "I knew it was coming, but I thought that maybe the Republicans would be better prepared this time around," Knoedler said. "They were talking a very tough game. But the thing is, on the Republican side, everybody that talks a tough game does not have money. The Democrats' side—you know the people that talk a tough game are...Ted Trimpa and Al Yates, and those guys really do have access to millions."

At one point, Knoedler said lobbyists told him a Democratic poll showed he had pulled even with Boyd in September. "So [CoDA] rebudgeted. You know, for them it's not how much money do we have, it's like how much money does it take? It's a totally different question," he said. "The mail just started pouring in."

Right before the absentee votes were cast, he was invited to the home of Alex Cranberg, an oil and gas executive and Colorado's preeminent school choice supporter. When he walked into the room, he saw "literally, the richest people in Colorado that are Republican...I'm talking about the richest—you know the hundreds-of-millionaires, not just the seventy-millionaires. I figured I was probably looking at a net worth in the room of about $2 billion and this was the concept the Dems had, but these people weren't donors to Trailhead."

The group questioned Knoedler and some of the other targeted candidates who were there to discuss their races. Knoedler told them the Dems had him tied—this is what he had raised, this is what he was doing to win and how he thought that could happen.

"I left realizing that all these guys wanted to hear...[was] that it's worth investing in Republicans this time around," he said. "But I think they looked at the numbers and...just assumed it's not going to work. It's not worth writing the check—and nobody wrote it."

When the results were tallied, the Democrats had gained four more seats in the House, for a 39–26 majority, and two more seats in the Senate, for a 20–15 majority. Boyd beat Knoedler 56–44, and they found themselves coincidentally seated in the same section at Boulder's Folsom Field the following Saturday for a University of Colorado football game.

The conversation was pleasant. After all, despite their differences on policy, Boyd and Knoedler shared a common bond that nobody else in Colorado could claim: they had just endured the most highly targeted legislative race in the state that year. Just as Knoedler had been hammered by CoDA, Boyd was beaten up by a smaller but no less aggressive campaign by Republican 527s.

As hard as both had worked, the reality was that Betty Boyd and Matt Knoedler were simply bit players in their own campaigns. They could have taken six-month vacations, left the country entirely, and most voters in their district wouldn't have known the difference. It was almost as if neither of them existed as people, but as biographies to be massaged, amplified, and distorted by powerful outsiders in slick campaign mailers and hard-edged television advertisements.

The most troubling thing for Republicans was the fact that CoDA's tactics in 2006 seemed to have an edge that hadn't been there in 2004. Nowhere was this more on display than in the House District 59 race 330 miles away from the Boyd-Knoedler contest.

On the eve of the 2006 election, Republicans in southwestern Colorado received a piece of mail that could have only come from the conservative wing of the party. On it, the Republican House candidate— Ellen Roberts—was attacked for being pro-choice.

Roberts had earned the right to represent the GOP on the November ballot. But like her predecessor, the term-limited Mark Larson, Roberts was a moderate Republican, sometimes out of favor with conservatives. In particular, her views on abortion galled some local GOP activists.

The anonymous oversized postcard was clearly intended to keep pro-life Republicans from voting for her. Yet, given the timing, the only person who could benefit from it was Roberts's Democratic opponent, Joe Colgan.

It seemed like déjà vu. Two years earlier, incumbent Republican House member Ramey Johnson had been hit with a last-minute Republican-funded mailer criticizing her for not supporting school choice. Days later, Johnson lost her race by forty-eight votes. And now it looked like the party was up to the same "circular firing squad" tactics.

Roberts went on to win her race, 52–48, but she was upset with some of her fellow Republicans. "A week after the election, she accused these [conservative] elements of a 'fratricide attempt' and called for the resignation of the county's party chairwoman," reported *The Durango Herald*.

Roberts began an investigation. The mailer had no return address, no indication of where it originated. Following the only available clue on the piece, she discovered a bombshell.

"Now Roberts says she has tracked the source of the flyer through the Salt Lake City–based bulk-mail permit number printed in small letters in one corner," *The Herald* reported. "She said she found the permit belongs to 360jmg, a communications firm with ties to the Clinton administration that trumpets its ads' roles in Democratic victories in the Colorado House."

The abortion mailer hadn't come from Republicans after all. Roberts had just been initiated into the new reality of legislative campaigns in Colorado circa 2006. Welcome to a brave new world.

If 2004 changed the game, 2006 blew it up. According to the *Rocky Mountain News*, the final amount spent on state races ended up being about $10.8 million on the Democratic side, compared to the Republicans' $6.4 million. As in 2004, most Democratic fundraising came from just a handful of large donors. Of the $10.8 million (which does not, it should be noted, include the money given to various non-527 CoDA nonprofits), Pat Stryker and Tim Gill accounted for about $3 million, with labor unions also contributing significant amounts. On the Republican side, the largest individual donors—businessmen Joel Farkas and Pete Coors—gave $200,000 each.

The Roundtable's $3.6 million for 2004 legislative races, a stunning figure at the time, was eclipsed by CoDA's commitment in 2006. According to the Center for Responsive Politics, CoDA's three legislative 527s raised over $7 million.

Since Republicans divided their field operations across Trailhead and the House and Senate 527s, there is no easy apples-to-apples comparison with Republican spending on legislative races. But to put the scope of the Democrats' 2006 state legislative program in perspective, it was almost $1 million more than Republican groups spent on all legislative races, two congressional races, and the gubernatorial race *combined*.

According to Burt Hubbard of the *Rocky Mountain News*, "Democratic and Republican independent groups poured $1.23 million into four key Senate races in just twenty days [in October]. That is almost double what the eight candidates for the four seats spent during their entire campaigns combined." In the other chamber, the *Rocky* reported, "Republican and Democratic 527 committees spent about $1.5 million in the first twenty-five days in October on 11 key state House races. That's one-and-a-half times what the candidates spent combined during their entire campaigns."

In all, CoDA-sponsored organizations facilitated over 600,000 pieces of mail, made over 300,000 phone calls, helped encourage 50,000 infrequent voters to the polls, and provided rides to roughly 1,300 voters.

When the dust settled, Democrats had expanded their margins in the state House and Senate and elected their first governor in eight years, Bill Ritter.

Colorado Democracy Alliance members congratulated themselves and reminded one another of one of their favorite quotes from humanitarian Margaret Mead: "Never doubt that a small group of thoughtful, committed citizens can change the world. Indeed, it's the only thing that ever has."

For his part, Ritter discounts the idea that money was the decisive factor in races like his and Knoedler's. "There has to be a product, and it has to be a product that consumers will buy, and so not any business model with funding is going to work," he said. "Funding is not the only thing. The group of people behind the efforts in 2004 and 2006 developed an understanding of where the state was and were able to exploit the vulnerabilities of the opponents. It's a combination of having a progressive agenda, good candidates, and a vulnerable opponent, plus a well-funded strategy. Those are the four things that worked together. If you take any one of those four things away, then I don't think that the strategy works."

For Ritter, the story is about expanding the size of the Democratic tent as much as it is expanding the number of donors. It's also about a Republican Party that's struggling with its identity.

"The [Republicans] are befuddled in part because they're wrestling for the soul of their defense. They don't know if they want to play with conservatives or if they want to play with moderates. They don't know if they should all be linebackers or if they should all be safeties. They don't have a sense of how to defend this because they, on the other side, have an ideological split that keeps them from being unified and really able to make their case to Coloradans.

"Since Ronald Reagan, there's really been a coalition in America of gun conservatives, tax conservatives, and social conservatives who have forgiven each other their trespasses. Where they didn't agree, they didn't bother. They weren't bothered by their lack of agreement because what they believed in was Republican rule. And as Republican rule did not deliver on the promise to those groups the way they wanted, they began to be more suspect of [their fellow Republicans].

"In Colorado, the social conservatives basically have not delivered on anything—Let me say it another way. The electorate has not been as receptive to the social conservatives because there are other, bigger, more meaningful issues than what appear to be the social issues that make up the social conservatives' main agenda. You can talk a lot about gay issues, about abortion, about things like this that I don't discount as being important issues, but if your roads are crumbling, your schools are falling down around you, and you have a healthcare system that's entirely broken, then people in this state are going to look to leadership and say, 'What are you doing?'

"And I think that's a part of this electorate being receptive to a progressive message...There are people in this state who are fiscally conservative, but they still want government to work. They're more pragmatic perhaps than the social conservatives are. And there's a group of independents and moderate Republicans who just quit forgiving the social conservatives for their trespasses because they weren't delivering on any other part of the agenda. Conversations at the state Capitol were largely about social issues and they were not moving on school funding, transportation funding, or finding ways to fix a broken healthcare system. That's been important to Democrats because our strategy is to talk about how you progress. What the future of this state looks like. What is it we can do to return to a place where Coloradans can be proud to be Coloradans?"

For Ritter's vanquished opponent Bob Beauprez, the takeaway is a lot simpler.

"They executed an extremely good plan," he said. "[General David] Petraeus should be as good of a field general as those guys obviously are. It's made it very difficult on our side because we don't have anything that comes close."

Chapter Fifteen

Taking It to the States Part Two:
Wisconsin and Texas in the Crosshairs

On the surface, Matt Angle, a progressive Texas Democrat, and Julaine Appling, a socially conservative Wisconsin Republican, seem to have little in common. But in 2008, each participated in the expansion of the Colorado blueprint to their respective states.

Angle is the director of the Texas Democratic Trust, a Colorado Democracy Alliance (CoDA)–like network with offices near the Texas state Capitol and in Washington, DC. Like Colorado Democrats before him, the former congressional staffer lives in a state dominated by Republicans. And like Colorado Democrats before him, he wants to shock the world by turning a red state blue.

The trust aims to help Democrats take control of the Texas state legislature by 2010. When its operations began in 2005, Republicans held an 87–63 majority in the Texas House. After the ballots were counted in 2008, that majority was 76–74. In the last two election cycles, six Democrats took Republican seats by fewer than 1,000 votes, thanks in large part to the coordinated effort conceived and executed by the trust. It was the same kind of strategic single-mindedness that helped vault Colorado Democrats into power.

Angle started with three large donors and now has roughly two dozen. He has directed resources to bolster the Texas Democratic Party's voter files on 12 million residents, to perform detailed polling, and to conduct microtargeted research to learn what Texans want and make sure they are hearing about the issues they care about.

Organizationally, the trust's structure bears remarkable resemblance to the network established by the Roundtable in Colorado in 2004 and perfected by CoDA in 2006. Internal documents show that the trust's advisory board includes the Texas House Democratic Campaign Committee, Texas Senate Democratic Caucus, Texas Trial Lawyers Association, Texas American Federation of Labor— Congress of Industrial Organizations, and the Texas State Teachers Association.

The trust's strategy to raise large contributions from a small universe of donors also mirrors the Colorado strategy, minimizing fund-raising efforts and allowing Angle and his team to channel their energy into getting results at the ballot box. "Colorado showed [us] how to go from venture capital to investment capital," Angle said. "By having a relatively small number of donors put up a relatively large amount of money, they showed that by investing in structure and strategy you can win. That allowed people like me to make the case [to donors] that this kind of project could pay off."

While Texas is significantly larger than Colorado, Angle's game plan is familiar. "Colorado gave us inspiration to fight back and be creative, and it showed that you could change the rules of engagement," he observed. "While we're doing it a little differently in Texas, it's with a similar intent."

Twelve hundred miles away, Appling is busy playing defense against a man whose name she didn't even know two years ago: Tim Gill. As the head of Wisconsin Family Action, she first heard about Gill in 2006, when he supported a group called Fair Wisconsin that sought to defeat a marriage amendment on the ballot that defined the institution as between a man and a woman. He had not played in that state's legislative elections at the time, but, as Appling said, "that changed in 2008."

Republicans held a 51–47 advantage, with one independent, in the state assembly heading into November. They knew their incumbents would be targeted, and polls showed a Democratic wave at the ballot box, but Wisconsin historically has been a state where voters favor people before party. Homespun candidates who grew up in communities represented them in Madison for long periods of time, even if their views didn't necessarily change with their neighbors.

Representative J. A. "Doc" Hines was one of those lawmakers. A veteran of World War II, the father of five was the oldest member of the legislature. He looked after his area's animals as a trained veterinarian and also found time to raise beef on his farm while simultaneously running a bed-and-breakfast in central Wisconsin. His district catered to those interests: agriculture and tourism. The landscape was dotted with dairy cows, clean lakes, and the Wisconsin Dells, the state's haven for Midwest families looking for summer fun at Lake Delton or one of the numerous water parks in the area.

The 42nd Assembly District had been held by a Republican for more than four decades, two of those belonging to former governor and US Health and Human Services secretary Tommy Thompson. It had been as reliably red as the outfit of Bucky Badger, the mascot at the state's flagship university.

During the 2006 election, which some Wisconsin Republicans called "The Great Republican Slaughter," Hines had actually increased his margin of victory, winning with 54 percent of the vote. Party activists had labeled his seat coming into the fall of 2008 as "the one we ought to keep." One state political blog said, "There's no such thing as a sure thing, but Doc's next best thing to it."

Hines's legislative history since he was first chosen in a special election in 2001 was reliably pro-gun (National Rifle Association A+ rating) and reliably pro–public health (he was complimented numerous times for his efforts to help pass a smoking ban, raise the tobacco tax, and require extra tests for drivers over seventy-five looking to renew their licenses) as the chairman of the assembly's public health committee.

The eighty-one-year-old Hines had not preached from any political pulpit about the topic of marriage and had even said publicly that same-sex couples could decide to live together and receive benefits.

But when it came to marriage per se, well, that was different. As he told the *Baraboo News Republic*, "I believe they should be allowed to live their lives without anybody bothering them. But I just don't believe that's what marriage is. As far as marriage, this is supposed to be between a man and a woman."

Those words were heard in Colorado. Soon, Hines's Democratic opponent, Fred Clark, began to receive the state-allowed maximum donation of $500 from benefactors living in places like Los Angeles, Seattle, New York, Chicago, Palm Springs, and Telluride, Colorado. Jon Stryker, Pat Stryker's brother, sent $500 from his home in Michigan. The Democratic challenger would eventually raise 20 percent more money than the Republican incumbent.

As if that weren't enough, copying another page from the Colorado playbook, a 527 called the Greater Wisconsin Committee, which described itself on its website as pursuing a "progressive policy agenda," bought television advertising on local cable outlets. The ad displayed the familiar catchphrase from the Bugs Bunny cartoon "What's Up, Doc Hines?" throughout the commercial while not-so-delicately twisting Hines's votes on state budget issues.

The Washington, DC–based firm that received $400,000-plus for producing the media in the campaign against Hines would be familiar to those following Colorado races: it was 360jmg, which produced mailers in Colorado legislative races in 2004 and 2006.

Hines would end up being trounced by Clark, 58–42, in November.

Appling said Hines's experience was not isolated, and she attributed it to a single software millionaire living in Colorado: Tim Gill.

"With the click of a mouse, Tim Gill can activate dozens of donors around the country to target competitive state and local races," she said, believing he coordinated contributions to seven legislative races that led to the flipping of the state Assembly's majority. "When he sends that e-mail, a flood of $250 checks and $500 checks start coming in."

"He did the calculations and said we've got to take X number of seats, and he did it. He's the wizard behind the curtain."

The wizard was at work in other states, too, just as he had been in 2006. In 2008, Gill's network targeted, among others, six seats in the Montana legislature and eighteen in New Mexico, helping to ensure victories in almost all. In just three election cycles, Gill had personally influenced more state legislative races in more states than perhaps any single person in American history.

Surveying the post-Gill political landscape, Appling has a message for her fellow conservatives: "The Colorado story shows what can happen when the average citizen doesn't pay attention to what's going on behind the curtain," she said. "These days, it doesn't take twenty-five years for a political transformation—it can take just a cycle or two to change a state dramatically. What happened in Colorado should put people on alert that a state's political leadership can be radically changed in a very short time."

Part Four
The Next Step

Chapter Sixteen

The Democracy Alliance:
The Colorado Model Goes National

As state-based donor groups like the Texas Democratic Trust are forming, national progressive donors have taken steps to jump-start similar efforts across the country. The hub of that activity is a secretive Washington, DC–based network called the Democracy Alliance.

Former Clinton administration staffer Rob Stein founded the alliance in 2005 as a response to conservative nonprofits like the Heritage Foundation, Cato Institute, and the American Enterprise Institute. Since then, he has received pledges from an estimated eighty donors, each agreeing to commit $1 million to fund Democracy Alliance initiatives. According to the conservative Capital Research Center (CRC), the Democracy Alliance's patrons include financier George Soros, the American Federation of Labor—Congress of Industrial Organizations, retired investment banker Steven Gluckstern, Progressive Casualty Insurance founder Peter Lewis, Taco Bell heir Rob McKay, Hollywood personalities Norman Lear and Rob Reiner, the Service Employees International Union, and a few names familiar to Coloradans: Rutt Bridges, Tim Gill, and Pat Stryker.

In structure and intent, the Democracy Alliance closely resembles the structure employed by Democrats to great effect in Colorado from 2004 to 2008. The similarities are not accidental.

According to *The Nation*, "The [Democracy Alliance] would not dole out money itself, but collectively the partners would meet twice a year through its auspices to decide which organizations to fund, forming working groups based on four priority areas: ideas, media, leadership and civic engagement. The working groups would present their recommendations to an investment committee made up of members of the board, who would pass them to the entire group. Partners would then give money [directly] to the organizations they favored, voting with their checkbooks. A Democracy Alliance recommendation meant a valuable gold star for prospective progressive organizations."

This is precisely the model adopted by the Roundtable in 2004 and refined by the Colorado Democracy Alliance in 2006, thanks in part to the input and strategic advice provided by Coloradans like Ted Trimpa (who is now a board member of the Democracy Alliance) and Al Yates (who helped found the Democracy Alliance). "Ted Trimpa and Al Yates, and others who have worked with them, represent a unique combination of political sophistication, management expertise, and collaborative style," Stein said. "They listen, they treat people with respect, and they are able to set aside their personal and ideological agendas for the greater common purpose."

Most of the Democracy Alliance's activities are nonpublic, but parts of its state-based strategy are beginning to emerge. In December 2008, Matthew Vadum of CRC published a detailed report describing the Democracy Alliance's efforts to "franchise their operations at the state level." Capital Research Center noted that grant data indicates that Democracy Alliance members "are heavily involved in financing Democrats" in Michigan, Minnesota, Ohio, and Wisconsin.

That's just the tip of the iceberg.

"There are three states that are head and shoulders above all the other states in terms of building a healthy, sustainable, progressive infrastructure," Stein told a group of insiders at the 2008 Democratic National Convention. "They are Colorado, Minnesota, and Wisconsin. And in all three of those states, they have structured donor alliances, fifteen or twenty or twenty-five individual and institutional donors, aggregating their money and putting it out in a strategic and coordinated way."

"In about ten other states, there are very serious donors who have just in the last six to twelve months come to the table. They've got political operatives working with them, and they are going to begin building in a very serious way in 2009 and beyond," he continued.

Rather than wait for state-based donor alliances to form, however, and perhaps to spur such activity, the Democracy Alliance has aggressively provided seed capital to build elements of progressive infrastructure in its target states.

These activities are difficult to track, since the Democracy Alliance makes recommendations to its members, who then directly donate to selected non-profits. In other words, there is no public record of the Democracy Alliance's priorities. But by linking common donors and organizations, Vadum has been able to identify over thirty nonprofits and networks of nonprofits that are likely affiliated with the Democracy Alliance.

Of those, three in particular appear linked to state-level organizations that have been used effectively in Colorado. They cover three critical infrastructure capacities the Democracy Alliance has sought to nurture: new media content generation (done through the Center for Independent Media), the capability to file legal actions against targeted officials and candidates and then generate publicity on the basis of those actions (done through the Center for Responsibility and Ethics, or CREW, in Washington), and grassroots organization (done through the ProgressNow network).

"We already know that CREW is a Democracy Alliance–approved grantee," said Vadum. "The fact that the Center for Independent Media and Progress-Now have donors in common and that the foundations giving them money are controlled by Democracy Alliance members strongly suggests that the Center for Independent Media and ProgressNow are Democracy Alliance–approved grantees as well."

The crown jewel of the Democracy Alliance's efforts is ProgressNow, a network of state-based organizations patterned on the Colorado-based nonprofit directed by original Roundtable member Michael Huttner.

When it started operations as the Rocky Mountain Progressive Network in 2003, it was initially mocked by conservatives. Huttner recalled being a guest on the show of popular Denver radio talk show host Mike Rosen. At the end of a contentious hour and a half of back and forth, Rosen ended the segment by saying, "Jared Polis, if you're listening, this may not have been a great investment on your part." Polis was listening and would have a good laugh later when he recalled that interview.

At the suggestion of Yates, the organization changed its name to ProgressNow. In its current form, ProgressNow gives progressives a long-term communications and grassroots capacity that can be mobilized to help Democrats when needed.

"It used to be a big problem on both sides, but especially the Left, in that they would put money in it during election years and then the day after the election everything would shut down, they would lose the voter file, they would lose the list, they would lose everybody," Huttner told Brad Jones of the conservative news organization Face the State in 2008.

ProgressNow changed that. "We wanted to set up a nonstop communications shop that would run all year long, not just during the election," Huttner said. "We wanted to distill the think tank research to talking points that were more understandable and then blogging. That's evolved into online organizing and networking."

By 2009, ProgressNow boasted an astonishing 375,000 e-mail addresses in Colorado, all of which could be contacted with the click of a mouse. With access to that many voters, ProgressNow has a direct line to the people who decide elections.

"Ultimately the commodity we're dealing with is political power," said Huttner. "It's all about building political power at the state level. We're trying to replicate our model in every state."

Since 2006, ProgressNow has launched affiliates in California (Courage Campaign), Florida (Progress Florida), Michigan (Progress Michigan), Minnesota (Alliance for a Better Minnesota), Nevada (ProgressNow Nevada), New Hampshire (Granite State Progress), New Mexico (Clearly New Mexico), Ohio (ProgressOhio), Pennsylvania (Keystone Progress), Washington (Fuse Washington), and Wisconsin (One Wisconsin Now). They aim to have a presence in twenty-five states by 2012.

ProgressNow acts as a clearinghouse for information that can then be pushed out through its networks. "The big hole in the progressive infrastructure that we filled was that in each state, we act almost like a PR firm to help all the different progressive organizations," Huttner told National Public Radio in 2008.

"We want to help grassroots activists use cutting-edge technology to mobilize and to help with message development to get earned media and encourage a progressive agenda," Huttner said. Huttner and ProgressNow affiliates wake up in the morning with one question on their minds: "How do we get earned media to advance our agenda and to criticize our opponents?"

The way it works is surprisingly simple. ProgressNow harvests e-mail addresses and personal contact information from voters year-round through their websites, and during election years they flip the switch on those networks to spread election messages attacking Republican candidates. If they're lucky, the press might pick up part of the message and report it as news.

"We'll put out a press release for the mainstream media, and then literally hours later we'll send out an e-mail on the same topic to tens of thousands of people," Huttner told National Public Radio. "The press actually get those e-mails sent to them. And then the press decides to write a story. And then when people read the story, they go to our website and even take further action."

Once on the site, visitors are urged to "Join the network!" by signing up for future e-mail notifications. They can also sign an online petition (perhaps for healthcare reform, or against "hate radio"), join a topical group (on clean energy or concealed weapons, for example), or enter their home address to generate a customized e-mail to their representatives in Congress or the state legislature.

Senator John McCain saw the result of how successful the model could be when videos taken by ProgressNow and its state partners in places like Ohio, Pennsylvania, and Colorado started popping up on YouTube alleging racism at McCain-Palin rallies.

Also in the campaign of 2008, the ProgressNow affiliate Alliance for a Better Minnesota bought nearly a million dollars worth of television time, according to Minnesota Public Radio, to run commercials attacking Minnesota Republican US senator Norm Coleman. Highlighting $4.00 gas at the pump, the ad stated, "Coleman votes to give oil and gas companies billions of dollars in tax breaks. Maybe that's why oil and gas interests have given Coleman hundreds of thousands of dollars in campaign contributions." Minnesota political analysts said the ads played a key role in Democrat Al Franken's razor-thin victory over Coleman.

Typically, ProgressNow's strategy is not so much to build up Democrats as it is to tear down Republicans, using opposition research and other hardball tactics. "We'll say things that are very critical," Huttner said. "We'll go after them very starkly and in a way that draws emotion. It's too hard hitting for some politicians to say these things, even if they really want someone else to say them."

Nor does ProgressNow try to tee up "October surprises"—the timed release of negative information just before the election, when it can inflict the maximum political damage. Understanding that the Web can perpetuate information indefinitely, ProgressNow will pull the trigger the instant it learns something that could harm the opposition.

"The moment we get research now, it goes out on the blogs," Huttner said. "It gets sent in an e-mail. The old campaigns would sit on their most explosive stuff until the two months before an election. We don't wait."

The Democratic base, and Senator Obama's campaign, took notice. Among the people Huttner worked with after starting ProgressNow were the founders of Blue State Digital, who put together the Democratic nominee's record-setting online fund-raising and organizational efforts. "Basically, we were the guinea pig for the Obama online platform," Huttner said.

When asked why Republicans have nothing like ProgressNow, Huttner's words almost sound like friendly advice to conservatives: "The truth is, there was something in the Republican mentality. They underestimated the importance of technology and tried to write it off as a liberal fad until Obama. Now they're trying to catch up. They've got a ways to go. These are tools that anyone can use and there's no reason these tools couldn't be used by right-wingers."

Chapter Seventeen

Election 2008:
For CoDA, No More Worlds to Conquer

On July 21, 2008, *Weekly Standard* subscribers opened their mailboxes to a dire prediction from one of the most trusted conservative voices in the country.

"The Democratic surge in Colorado reflects the national trend, but it involves a great deal more," wrote Fred Barnes. "There's something unique going on in Colorado that, if copied in other states, has the potential to produce sweeping Democratic gains nationwide."

There had already been several articles in *The Atlantic, Time, The Nation, The New Republic*, and other publications largely focusing on the influence of Tim Gill, Pat Stryker, and others. But Barnes was the first national figure to sound the alarm to the conservative base that this story was no mere curiosity—it was a matter of political survival.

"With enough money, its main elements can no doubt be replicated in other states," he wrote. "But a large measure of political shrewdness and opportunism is also required, political traits that have eluded Republicans in Colorado while becoming the hallmark of their opponent."

Barnes told his readers about an internal campaign memo leaked to the *Rocky Mountain News* in January that purportedly laid out an $11.7 million budget for its 527 networks to destroy Bob Schaffer, the Republican candidate for US Senate, and incumbent US representative Marilyn Musgrave. He wrote that the money was coming from "rich liberal donors."

The memo articulated that there would be a multimillion-dollar advertising campaign in March and April to "define Schaffer/foot on throat." Its author told the *Rocky Mountain News* that the page marked *Confidential* was simply "a document to give to prospective clients, and that's all I can say."

Barnes labeled the tactics clever and dubbed the overarching scope of the progressive efforts the "Colorado Model." He predicted it would be a "major topic of discussion when Democrats convene in Denver in the last week of August for their national convention."

He was right.

Since 2003, when Governor Howard Dean was a presidential candidate, Dean had seen the promise of Colorado, telling reporters outside the University of Colorado at Boulder that "the road to the White House goes through the Rocky Mountain West." The success Colorado Democrats had achieved since his campaign famously croaked after an ill-timed inflexion issue in Iowa was patterned, in part, on Dean's online infrastructure.

When Dean was named to run the party, he saw an opportunity to highlight a state's success and vindicate some of his own philosophies in the process by giving the Democratic National Convention (DNC) to Denver. In fact, his Internet guru, Bobby Clark, came to Colorado to join ProgressNow with Michael Huttner after the Dean campaign concluded. By the summer of 2008, their database held the names and e-mails of nearly 2.5 million voters.

On the day before Senator Barack Obama accepted his party's nomination at the DNC, Clark participated in a panel that ProgressNow set up for bloggers covering the convention. He discussed "Netroots: Past, Present, Future" with some of the preeminent people in progressive politics: Eli Pariser, the executive director of MoveOn.org; Markos Moulitsas, founder of Daily Kos; and Christy Hardin-Smith, a blogger at FireDogLake.com.

The other forum featuring Colorado that day was called "Democracy Alliance: Colorado as a Model" and took place at the Starz Green Room. In the audience were two of the men who shaped the change in Colorado: Rutt Bridges and Al Yates. Colorado Democracy Alliance (CoDA) executive director Laurie Hirschfeld Zeller took the opportunity to stress the importance of unity in CoDA's success.

"If you want people in office, if you want someone in office that exactly meets all of your criteria, that fits all of your values, that mirrors what you deeply believe, then run for office," said Zeller. "But the reality of it is that you have to find ways to elect people who will support most of what you care about. And you have to be a little forgiving. It has to be a larger tent. You can't have a whole string of litmus tests about what it means to be a progressive."

Unity and coordination were essential, but the element of surprise had been key to CoDA's smashing victories. And to preserve that, secrecy was vital.

Zeller told the crowd that for CoDA to "remain effective and agile, we have had to try and be discreet about our efforts. There's a playbook here that you don't want to leave on the table in a Starbucks."

Unfortunately for CoDA, its playbook had been left on a copy machine. A month after the DNC panel, a conservative news organization, Face the State, revealed dozens of confidential internal documents detailing CoDA's structure, membership, and strategies from the 2006 election. The documents had been picked up by Isaac Smith, a thirty-year-old intern for Bridges's now-defunct Bighorn Policy Center.

Smith, an unaffiliated voter who had recently completed a master's degree in public administration, sat on the documents for nearly a year before releasing them. After several local media outlets passed on the story, Face the State posted them on its website, turning the Colorado political world inside out.

The most controversial document was a memo identifying CoDA's plans to "Educate the Idiots," a union get-out-the-vote campaign targeting "minorities, GEDs, dropouts," and others. That memo was quickly labeled as a fake by CoDA officers and its lawyer, but Face the State's report was linked by *The Drudge Report* and 100,000 page views later, the political world finally got a peek at the inner workings of CoDA, an organization that operated so secretly, even its name was unknown beyond a small circle of insiders.

All the while, the progressive machine continued to work smoothly. After the success of the Both Ways Bob campaign in 2006, ProgressNow turned its attention to Colorado's last major political position not yet in the hands of progressives, the sole GOP US Senate seat. With Republican senator Wayne Allard honoring a pledge to return to Colorado after two terms, the race was being watched nationwide.

The Democrats put up Representative Mark Udall, a veteran congressman from the Boulder area whose family has been described as the "Kennedys of the West." The Republicans countered with former Representative Bob Schaffer, who honored his own term-limits pledge and left Congress voluntarily in 2003.

It was Schaffer's job after he left Congress that drew ProgressNow's and its executive director, Michael Huttner's, attention. Schaffer went to work for Aspect Energy, a Denver-based company whose portfolio included largely traditional forms of energy (i.e., oil and natural gas) and had just started projects in renewable forms. As gas prices rose early in 2008, the nickname "Big Oil Bob" and the corresponding website, www.bigoilbob.com, came naturally to some, even though Huttner wasn't sold immediately.

"I didn't like it right away because I thought it limited our options to criticize him," said Huttner, "but it became about him being seen as corrupt. It was an ethics thing, not an energy issue."

ProgressNow sounded the alarm to its 375,000-member e-mail list and its comprehensive list of media contacts. Every news release, every statement out of Schaffer's mouth was countered with an e-mail calling him Big Oil Bob. The moniker made it into the newspapers and the League of Conservation Voters (whose senior vice president for political affairs is original Roundtable member Tony Massaro) began running television advertisements hammering it home. ProgressNow's job was done.

Udall rolled to victory (56–44) and Schaffer publicly wondered, as Bob Beauprez did two years earlier, how he was always on the defensive and why his campaign never gained traction.

Huttner's tactics are equally groused about and respected by his Republican counterparts.

"I'm a big fan," said Sean Duffy, who was the deputy chief of staff to Republican governor Bill Owens. "When I was in the governor's office, he started to send us open-records requests for everything, like what toothpaste the governor was buying. Basically, he brought an East Coast offense out here to the West—an intense, no-deference-shown, aggressive form of politics...When I moved out here from Pennsylvania (where I worked for Governor Tom Ridge), I was astonished [by] how genteel politics were out here. Huttner brought a New York, Pennsylvania, New Jersey, [and] even national take to the game...

"Huttner will do anything—dress in a pea pod suit—anything to get attention, and I say that with all respect. He'll hammer away. If he gets five cameras, great. If he gets one camera, he doesn't care. He gets attention for his views, and also he gets to say to all their supporters, 'We're standing up for our team.'

It's a motivational tool for their base."

Yet Huttner is but one part of a larger effort. When all of CoDA's elements join together in pursuit of a common goal, the network becomes much more than the sum of its parts. Perhaps no episode illustrates that fact better than the case of Republican US representative Marilyn Musgrave, who ran into the CoDA buzzsaw in three subsequent election cycles before ultimately succumbing to Democrat Betsy Markey in 2008.

For years, Colorado Democrats hoped to unseat Musgrave. She was out of touch, they argued, pushing conservative social issues while the nation fought a war on terrorism, struggled with increasing energy prices, and began to experience the pains of a slowing economy.

At the heart of Democratic passion was Musgrave's attempt to ban gay marriage through an amendment to the US Constitution. For Gill and Stryker in particular, taking out Musgrave became a matter of personal interest (Stryker, who lived in Musgrave's district, has a gay brother who lives in Michigan).

In 2004, the Roundtable funded 527 ads showing an actress in a pink suit perpetrating foul deeds. The ads were so aggressive that *The New York Times* gave one a "simpleton award" for being an "intelligence-insulting attack ad."

"It opens in a funeral parlor, where a blond woman in a pink suit (the blond congresswoman?) sneaks up to the open coffin," *The Times* editorial board wrote. "She strips the corpse of his wristwatch—the arm flops back down—as the voiceover gravely intones that Ms. Musgrave supported full payment of people's nursing home bills 'even after they're dead.'

"That's six-feet-under low, but wait—there's another anti-Musgrave ad depicting an American soldier feverishly firing his rifle at the enemy. Sure enough, just as the voiceover accuses the congress-woman of shortchanging the troops, there's that woman in pink, creeping up behind the soldier and picking his pocket to snatch money from his wallet."

Musgrave held on to win in 2004, but she was wounded.

In September 2005, the Center for Responsi-bility and Ethics (CREW) released a report entitled "Beyond Delay: The 13 Most Corrupt Members of Congress." Among the eleven Republicans and two Democrats named by the report was Musgrave, who happened to be preparing for a spirited and Stryker-backed opponent in Democratic state representative Angie Paccione the following year.

CREW's report was immediately picked up by the mainstream press. Calling CREW a watchdog group, publications like the *Chicago Tribune* and *The Seattle Times* reported CREW's findings without analysis. But back in Musgrave's district, the *Greeley Tribune* ran a more detailed article under the title "Musgrave Discred-its Corrupt Charges." The *Greeley Tribune* went on to report the substance of the accusation, namely that an office used in her previous election campaign "either doesn't exist or is part of her district office leased with public funds, which would be against the law."

The *Tribune* investigated further and found that Musgrave's campaign office, which did indeed exist, happened to be in a different suite in the same building as her district office and was paid with campaign funds under a separate lease. "It's just simply a political ploy," the *Tribune* quoted Musgrave's chief of staff, Guy Short, as saying about the CREW allegation.

But thanks to coordination among the various progressive groups with common donors, the discredited corruption story took on a life of its own. As the 2006 election heated up, ProgressNow posted a link to a video with a woman in a pink suit claiming to be Musgrave boasting that "I was labeled one of the thirteen most corrupt members of Congress, and I have well-known ties to corruption in the GOP by keeping money I received from the scandal-ridden likes of Tom DeLay and others linked to convicted lobbyist Jack Abramoff."

"Don't forget to forward this video on to your friends and family and anyone you know who lives in Marilyn's district," ProgressNow urged its members. The next day, Center for Independent Media affiliate *Colorado Confidential* (now known as *The Colorado Independent*) posted a link pushing its readers to the video.

Musgrave went on to win, but the allegation that she was one of the thirteen most corrupt members of Congress still wouldn't die. In the 2008 election cycle, it surfaced again when a nonprofit 527 called Defenders of Wildlife Action Fund (Stryker was a principal donor) ran a television advertisement stating, among other things, that "[Musgrave] was named one of the most corrupt members of Congress." Denver's KUSA television station investigated the ad and reported the *Greeley Tribune*'s findings that the claim, which at this point had been kept alive for over three years, was untrue.

After being bruised in 2004 and 2006, Musgrave was set up for the kill in 2008. "Millionaire gay-rights champions Tim Gill and Pat Stryker have funded groups that have attacked Musgrave from all sides," reported *The Denver Post*. "Soft-money organizations have spent twice as much fighting Musgrave as supporting her. The Defenders of Wildlife Action Fund alone has dropped $1.5 million to oppose Musgrave since September, according to Federal Election Commission records. Musgrave's biggest outside champion, the NRCC [National Republican Congressional Committee], has spent $980,000 in that time, according to FEC reports and committee statements."

The negativity led numerous voters to complain to their local television stations to "stop the noise" and plead for a "none of the above" category.

Musgrave refused to be a victim, accusing her opponent, first-time office-seeker Betsy Markey, of breaking the law during numerous commercials and public appearances. In one ad, she hooked up "Betsy Markey" to a polygraph test to "prove" she was lying to voters.

When asked during a debate televised on C-SPAN if there was anything she wished she would have done differently in her life, Musgrave told viewers she would have "defended myself faster once I was attacked."

In the end, the money, her record, and the anti-Republican political environment finally cost Musgrave her job. She would later blame her loss on "leftist special interests" that "overwhelmed us with money and...smothered the truth with vicious attacks and lies." Markey, meanwhile, attributed her victory to discussing the issues her district was interested in: jobs, energy, and healthcare rather than gay marriage and other social issues.

"It's kind of a whack a mole for Republicans here," said GOP consultant Sean Duffy. "You whack Huttner, up pops Chantell Taylor [of Colorado Ethics Watch]. You whack her, and up pops Colorado Media Matters. There's always another one popping up to keep you busy."

Jon Caldara, president of the conservative/libertarian Independence Institute, agrees. "A fully integrated scandal-manufacturing machine" is how he describes the interaction of the network's organizations. "The Democrats have outsourced the politics of personal destruction to a bunch of nonprofits."

In trendy lower downtown Denver, a few CoDA-affiliated nonprofits—including Colorado Conservation Voters, the Latina Initiative, and ProgressNow—share office space in a 100-year-old redbrick building. Known as the Alliance Center, the renovated warehouse has been celebrated for its certification from the US Green Building Council's Leadership in Energy and Environmental Design (LEED) program.

The Alliance Center boasts another distinction. According to the Alliance for Sustainable Colorado's website, the building's tenants successfully advanced over forty-five bills during the 2009 session of the Colorado General Assembly.

Visitors to the Alliance Center's lobby are greeted with an Ethiopian proverb: "When spider webs unite," it reads, "they can tie up a lion."

Chapter Eighteen

The Aftermath:
Money, Message, and a
New Blueprint for Victory

When the polls closed in Colorado in November 2008, the landscape of what a decade earlier had been considered one of the safest Republican states had shifted. Democrats, not Republicans, controlled the governor's mansion, both US Senate seats, five of seven congressional seats, and both chambers of the Colorado state legislature. Even Gang of Four member Jared Polis reaped the rewards, winning election to his first term in the US House of Representatives as a new congressman from Boulder.

Since then, Colorado Republicans have had plenty of time for reflection. How, they ask, could we have lost so much so quickly?

Money almost always comes up. "The beauty of Colorado is that it's big enough to be important but small enough that just a few people can radically change the political landscape," notes Jon Caldara. "It's the best bang for the buck in American politics."

Caldara clearly understands the game has changed—and that Republicans must adapt to the new environment to survive. "To win, you need to win the battle of ideas and put foot soldiers on the ground. And you can't do that without a long-term infrastructure. The Left understood much earlier [than Republicans] that the party no longer has anything to do with campaigns," Caldara said. "By building infrastructure outside the party, Democrats gained a huge advantage over Republicans. All of the Democratic funders were very tech savvy. They understood the power of Web-based communications. They figured if they could do this with fewer, bigger donors, they'd be left alone to focus on the mission."

He is quick to emphasize the latter point, noting that large but not overly involved donors are the key to establishing a lasting infrastructure. It is, he argues, a major reason progressives are light-years ahead of their conservative counterparts. "Republicans don't have principled, egoless financial leaders like Tim Gill and Pat Stryker who are willing to provide long-term investments," he said. "They were, in a way, political venture capitalists. The Left's donors set up organizations, didn't micromanage them, and let them do their jobs."

Former Republican congressman Tom Tancredo sees no reason why Republicans couldn't do the same things Democrats did, and with the same success. "It doesn't matter whether you are running for the state legislature or president of the United States," he observes. "Brilliant organization, unlimited resources, and the effective use of technology all in the hands of bright people who are driven by more than just simple ideology create the most formidable campaign strategy imaginable."

Meanwhile, the techniques used by Colorado progressives are being replicated, supersized, and exported across the nation.

In the summer of 2009, a Democracy Alliance–funded data mining firm called Catalist circulated an after-action report on the 2008 election cycle. The report, called "Aggregate Activities of Progressive Organizations in 2008," summed up the discernible impacts of more than ninety progressive organizations around the country.

The report began by conceding the obvious: "The 2008 election was about the candidacy of Barack Obama." Yet beneath the powerful rhythms of national dynamics, Catalist's report went on to demonstrate tangible, measurable ways in which progressive organizations were able to enhance and expand the margins in Democratic victories through scientific modeling and regression analysis. The metrics clearly showed the impact of the coordinated efforts of progressive organizations operating under the Democracy Alliance umbrella.

"Across the country," the report stated, "we see a very strong correlation between progressive victories and intense progressive activities." In particular, "progressive contact [including mail, phone calls, and paid canvassers] led to increases in turnout when controlling for predicted turnout based on past elections." The effectiveness of such efforts was especially true at the state and local level. "When controlling for demographic factors," the report concluded, "progressive activities still appear to explain outcome at the county level in a way that demographics alone cannot."

Catalist was, in many ways, the hub of voter outreach activities. With a data set of 260 million person records, Catalist maintains what is likely the largest and most detailed voter file in the country. For a fee, Catalist makes its national database available to progressive organizations, which in turn gathered individualized data about voters, helping to update and expand Catalist's database. Catalist's website notes that in the past, progressives often gathered data on an ad hoc basis, discarding it after an election. Until Catalist, national progressives lacked "an affordable and consistent data repository." But thanks to funding from the Democracy Alliance's donors, those records "are stored by Catalist, [and] improved with the new information gathered year in and year out, and through election cycles."

Catalist is the ultimate evolution of the fledgling data-sharing efforts pioneered by Colorado progressives in 2004.

In 2008, Catalist customers made over 127 million contacts to more than 49 million unique individuals. Of those, 28 million voted on Election Day. That represented 20 percent of all votes cast in the country. Eighty-two percent of these activities occurred in just sixteen highly contested states, such as Colorado, Florida, Indiana, North Carolina, Ohio, and Pennsylvania. They gathered "over 60 million pieces" of data from voters about their issues, their concerns, and their desires. "The data assets are being stored and mined for the future," the report states, "rather than being tossed in the trash."

Progressive activity expanded into states that had not been targeted in the past, and "down-ballot races" in states such as Alabama, Kentucky, and Louisiana showed the "emergence of progressive activities" as a result.

Finally, progressive groups registered more than 5.5 million new voters, 3.8 million of whom cast ballots. Catalist's report conservatively figures that if 60 percent voted for Senator Barack Obama, the number of new voters generated by progressive organizations provided more than the margin for victory in both Indiana and North Carolina.

The Colorado Model has gone big-time.

About the same time the Catalist report began to circulate, Fred Barnes returned to Colorado to once again discuss the state of the Colorado Model for a lecture series sponsored by the conservative, Washington, DC–based Heritage Foundation (ironically, one of the nonprofits the Democracy Alliance patterned its efforts after).

In the speech, entitled "How the Left Hijacked Colorado," Barnes once again assailed "rich liberals" for being behind one of the most dramatic state political turnarounds in recent American history.

ProgressNow founder Michael Huttner went to listen to Barnes's talk. The brainchild of he and many others was, after all, the subject of the speech.

"The Colorado Model, as many of you know, was an idea of putting an infrastructure of liberal organizations into a state as a test case to see if they could really push politics to the left and make a state that wasn't a liberal Democratic state a liberal Democratic state," Barnes said.

Democrats, Barnes argued, have "capitalized on this anti-Republican, anti-Bush, anti-conservative trend. Obviously, it's been the mood of the country that has affected elections in Colorado. But I believe so has this infrastructure of liberal organizations funded by rich people."

After the speech, Huttner called his colleague Alan Franklin and told him about Barnes's message.

Franklin chafed at the suggestion that it was all about the money. "[The Republicans] lost because they were on the wrong side of history," he wrote on the ProgressNow website afterward. "They lost because the voters of Colorado decided the 'solutions' conservatives were offering to the state's growing challenges weren't working. They lost because when the people of Colorado went to the conservatives for answers on issues like education and healthcare, they were given tax-cut rhetoric and diatribes about gay people. They lost because they were no longer effectively representing the people of Colorado."

But when it came to the role of outside groups in elections, Franklin gave credence to part of Barnes's thesis. "All that was missing," Franklin wrote of the Colorado progressive movement, "was permanent infrastructure."

Huttner left that night confident that his side still held the strategic edge over their Republican counterparts—and he could prove it with a souvenir. In his possession was a cover of the July 21, 2008, *Weekly Standard* with a headline of "The Colorado Model: Fred Barnes on the Democrats' plan for turning red states blue."

Beneath the headline was an autograph and personal note to Huttner: "To Michael: Keep the faith! Fred Barnes."

Barnes had stood inches from one of the architects of the Colorado Model and had no idea who Michael Huttner was.

Huttner's still smiling today.

And as for the signed magazine cover?

It's now framed and hanging on his office wall.

Epilogue

As this book goes to press, the blueprint devised by Colorado progressives and exported to other states faces the greatest challenge of its five-year existence. What was once a tailwind helping Democrats has reversed, and Republicans now feel that wind at their backs heading into the 2010 election cycle. One need look no further than Massachusetts to understand how the environment has changed from 2006 and 2008.

Yet if the blueprint is anything, it is about a lasting, sustainable infrastructure, a levee that should withstand—indeed, is designed to withstand—the natural highs and lows of the political cycle. As former Colorado Republican Party executive director (and current Republican National Committee regional political director) Alan Philp put it, "The infrastructure the Democrats manufactured in Colorado helps them to maximize their electoral gains in favorable political environments and minimize their losses in negative environments."

The growth of outside spending in elections is not going away; if anything, we can expect more. The recent US Supreme Court decision in *Citizens United v. Federal Election Commission* invalidated portions of federal campaign finance law that prohibit certain kinds of political spending by corporations and labor unions. The percentage of political advertisements coming from candidates and political parties will continue to diminish, with the balance

being supplied by political nonprofit entities possess-
ing vaguely appealing names that offer no clue as to
who, or what, is behind them.

Back in Colorado, outside groups long ago figured out how to circumvent contribution limits to
candidates and political parties by using nonprofits, so the *Citizens United* decision isn't expected to
change the environment much. Nor will the balance
of political power in the Centennial State, hopes ProgressNow's Michael Huttner. "I believe Colorado's
progressive infrastructure will work as a buttress
[against] the potential tidal wave against Democrats
in November," he says.

But Huttner also hedges his bets. "Having
said that," he adds, "it's only a buttress and if the
economy is not better come the fall of 2010, Colorado could also end up being subject to the cycles
of political history, which has shown time and time
again that citizens will vote against incumbents if
the perception is that they are no better off personally, especially in their pocketbook, than they were
in November 2008."

Afterword

In Their Own Words

Why Colorado Matters

"The beauty of Colorado is that it's big enough to be important but small enough that just a few people can radically change the political landscape. It's the best bang for the buck in American politics."

—Jon Caldara,
president of the Independence Institute

"We are fundamentally an independently minded state, a pretty moderate state. As the Republican Party went further to the right, it really opened the door to moderate Democrats—people like Ken Salazar, Bill Ritter—to be popular and win statewide. And really, we've never had a problem with people considering Democrats for our state and local offices. Even in districts that are traditionally Republican, where Bush won handily, people are open-minded and willing to check different party ballots."

—Jared Polis,
US representative (D-CO)

The Impact of Campaign Finance Reform

"I don't think it's a necessarily good system when the ground troops cannot talk to the air support, and that's basically what 527s end up being...air support. They see you getting beat up. You legally cannot have a conversation with them. And you can't comingle funds. You have to err on the side of staying away from them completely, which means they get to decide the message."

—Bill Ritter,
Colorado governor (D)

"State legislative races used to be local campaigns. They did revolve around a lot of local issues, and candidates were seen through that prism. But now they've basically become nationalized. There now is a statewide theme to these legislative races, and I think that's sad because I think people are voting on state legislative candidates now without having the foggiest idea of who the candidates are from the standpoint of who they are in their community, what they've done, what their thoughts are about local issues. I think that's been one of the casualties of this process as well."

—Dick Wadhams,
Colorado GOP chairman

"I'm a supporter of campaign finance reform. I think it's a better climate. It's not positive to have the candidate out there asking for money from people that are affected by the laws they are going to be making. Absolutely, by taking it on the outside, it's better than it was before when the candidates had to raise the money...It comes down to who is a candidate talking to. If you're only talking to people who are going to donate $2, $3, $4,000, you're talking to a very select slice of the American people, and they clearly have their own agenda. Even if it's not quid pro quo, and it's most often not, most people are not corrupt, it's just who you're hanging with, who you're talking to, who's at your fund-raisers, so I would love a system that encouraged small contributions, $25, $50, with federal matching funds."

—Jared Polis,
US representative (D-CO)

"[The rise of outside funding] is frustrating to candidates. At least it should be if it isn't. I wouldn't want somebody I don't know speaking for me. I think the other thing is, people are so burned out on politics you're not getting the really good people. You're getting the fringe on both sides. And I blame both parties there."

—Norma Anderson,
former Colorado state senator (R)

"We've learned that campaign finance reform doesn't work. Amendment 27 was designed to benefit Democratic candidates. Through loopholes that were put there by design, organized labor enjoys special exemptions from campaign finance limits. Colorado's campaign finance reform—which I opposed—was a significant part of the Democratic strategy to defund Republican candidates and empower their super-wealthy donors. It left huge loopholes for Democrats and tied the hands of traditional Republican supporters.

—Bill Owens,
former Colorado governor (R)

"Campaign finance reform has been a total failure. It has greatly enhanced 527s and shifted campaigns away from the candidates and their campaign managers."

—Robert Loevy,
professor, Colorado College

Did Democrats Win...Or Republicans Lose?

"The Republican Party in Colorado and nationally became beholden to a closed-minded constituency who opposed equality and motivates their base through fear. It's important to break that grip, and I look forward to a day when gay-baiting isn't a political party principle."

—Tim Gill,
businessman and donor

"Starting in the early 1990s, a civil war started within our party between moderates and conservatives that over time resulted in Democrats winning state legislative seats that historically had been Republican. Several moderate Republican incumbents found themselves fending off or even being defeated by conservative challengers. Although abortion certainly dominated these primaries, gun rights and fiscal issues also figured prominently. These primaries were so viciously fought that it often drove moderates to support Democrats in the general election or found conservatives just not voting at all in a race with a moderate Republican candidate, resulting in Democratic wins.

"I do not oppose primaries in general. Primaries can stir interest in a party and make candidates and campaigns sharper and more effective. But the scorched-earth primaries of the 1990s and early 2000s were deadly to our party. Fortunately, there has been little of this civil war [within the Republican Party] over the past couple of election cycles. I truly believe that Colorado Republicans have, by and large, moved beyond these fights as we find ourselves in such a minority position in the legislature."

—Dick Wadhams,
Colorado GOP chairman

"Conversations at the state Capitol were largely about social issues and they were not moving on school funding, transportation funding, or finding ways to fix a broken healthcare system. That's been important to Democrats because our strategy is to talk about how you progress, what the future of this state looks like, what is it we can do to return to a place where Coloradans can be proud to be Coloradans."

—Bill Ritter,
Colorado governor (D)

"Unfortunately, our 'conservative' leadership at both the national and state levels lost their way. Our Republicans in Washington grew government and spent more money. They pushed for amnesty for illegal immigrants and expanded the federal bureaucracy through programs like No Child Left Behind. Here in Colorado, Governor Owens pushed for tax increases and would not work with Republican legislators on issues like illegal immigration. All of these things disenfranchised and demoralized our base. At the same time, Democrats had an incredibly well-funded and organized operation that we couldn't compete with. It created a perfect storm."

—Ted Harvey,
Colorado state senator (R)

"The divisive primaries have reflected the split in the Republican Party between social conservatives and economic conservatives. The shift of upscale, inner-suburban, well-educated Republicans, mainly in Jefferson and Arapahoe counties, to the Democrats is the major change in Colorado politics at the present time. If a state has few social conservatives to be gained, social conservative domination of the Republican Party leads to major defections of old inner-suburban economic Republicans to the Democrats. This already happened in New England and Middle Atlantic states such as Connecticut and New Jersey, and is happening now in New Hampshire. Colorado is just catching up."

—Robert Loevy,
professor, Colorado College

"Democrats won with equal parts spectacular Democratic strategy, massive funding, and Republican implosion."

—Jon Caldara,
president of the Independence Institute

"Republicans have forgotten that politics is a game of addition, not subtraction."

—Norma Anderson,
former Colorado state senator (R)

Money or Message?

"They [Democrats and their donors] effectively bought the state. I can point to a series of individual state House and Senate races where their money helped turn the legislature Democratic. There were other factors at play, but the key difference was their overwhelming and dominant financial advantage."

—Bill Owens,
former Colorado governor (R)

"It would be great if they believed that [it's about money] because maybe that's why we've been able to continue [our success]. Because if that's what they think it is, they're clearly missing the mark and they're not likely to correct their course. And that's fine with me...It's not just resources. In fact, it could have been done with less resources, looking by the margins we won by in a lot of these races, but the story is where the political mainstream is, where the candidates are, how hard they work. It's what issues the Democratic and Republican leadership respectively focus on when they're in charge."

—Jared Polis,
US representative (D-CO)

"I'd left my job to run for office. In mid-October, the mail started flying. The pieces said all these horrible things about me. Here I have no job, and these multimillionaires are spending a bottomless pit of money to say bad things about me. We had no money in the bank. [It was] just crazy. The main thing that was scary about it was the dichotomy: I had no money, and these guys just said: 'Oh, yeah, what's his name? Knoedler? Here's $250,000.'"

—Matt Knoedler,
former Republican candidate for the Colorado state Senate

The Power of Infrastructure

"It's about creating an organization that worked effectively together across agenda lines to promote a common idea. There are certain things we value in this state. It brought together lots of elements, diverse voices, but there is an overarching shared vision. It's like the way Henry Ford decided people would want cars and he had to decide what's the most efficient, effective way to get them to the people."

—Bill Menezes,
former head of Colorado Media Matters

"Our job is to build a long-term progressive infrastructure in Colorado while we're conceding nothing in the short term, in terms of progressive goals at the ballot box. We provide services to our members in terms of research, advice on their giving, activating their collective interaction, to help make the progressive sector stronger. But our role is really to harness the financial resources as well as the brains and the energy of the progressive sector. And I want to stress that it's not just individual donors. One of the things that has been crucial in making the work of the Colorado Democracy Alliance effective in Colorado has been our partnership with institutional donors and activists organizations, labor particularly. That's been a major part of how we get our work done here."

—Laurie Hirschfeld Zeller,
former executive director of Colorado Democracy Alliance

"Republicans don't have principled, egoless financial leaders like Tim Gill and Pat Stryker who are willing to provide long-term investments. They were, in a way, political venture capitalists. The Left's donors set up organizations, didn't micromanage them, and let them do their jobs. Republicans don't have the patience or outlook to do that. Republican donors need to sever their contributions from candidates, who come and go in every campaign cycle, and instead use them to build a lasting infrastructure...The Right gets mesmerized by personalities. But to win, you need to win the battle of ideas and put foot soldiers on the ground. And you can't do that without a long-term infrastructure."

—Jon Caldara,
president of the Independence Institute

The Role of Technology

"The truth is, there was something in the Republican mentality. They underestimated the importance of technology and tried to write it off as a liberal fad until Obama. Now they're trying to catch up. They've got a ways to go...Basically, we were the guinea pig for the Obama online platform. We want to help grassroots activists use cutting-edge technology to mobilize and to help with message development to get earned media and encourage a progressive agenda. We are riding the wave of cutting-edge technology."

—Michael Huttner,
founder and CEO of ProgressNow

"All of the Democratic funders were very tech savvy. They understood the power of Web-based communications. They figured if they could do this with fewer, bigger donors, they'd be left alone to focus on the mission."

—Jon Caldara,
president of the Independence Institute

"Raising the level of [the Republican] game also means we have to upgrade the machinery of our campaigns—that means better operations, better organization, better tactics. For starters, we need to figure out that it's the Internet, not the Internets, and it doesn't bite. Our inability to successfully deploy technology in a world where information is disseminated by the latest gadget is, in my view, the modern-day equivalent of Nixon sweating during his TV debate with Kennedy. Nixon didn't know what worked in that emerging medium, and we certainly aren't very good at the emerging tools of information in today's tech-heavy world. This technology deficit is not decisive, but man, it sure does hurt our chances a lot. So we've got to improve our methods even as we sharpen our message. The same is true of our operations and organizations. Believing like Ronald Reagan doesn't mean we should run a campaign like he did."

—Josh Penry,
Colorado state Senate minority leader (R)

Can Colorado Republicans Come Back?

"You will not be able to beat this model through your Republican Party. This is beyond party. The only way to fight this is to put in a better infrastructure with long-term, multiyear objectives. This mind-set of raising money from a few rich guys in the final months of a campaign is a sure loser. And if your Republicans don't act like principled, limited-government fiscal conservatives, they will lose...Republican donors are too short-sighted and too micromanaging. They don't have a long-term vision, and they keep giving money to candidates instead of organizations that will still be there after the election. Republicans need to learn that Election Day is not the end of the fight."

—Jon Caldara,
president of the Independence Institute

"If you start with the basic concept that [politics] isn't rocket science, the technology available to everyone is the same, and the access to resources is about the same, then it comes back to some basic concepts. It's where the candidate recruitment and the policies you're promoting really do come into play. The Republicans often talk about issues that people don't care about every day, and that is where the disconnect has been. They always look for wedge issues, and voters care about quality healthcare for their families, their kids' education, and how their bills will get paid."

—Beth Ganz,
former head of America Votes

"It doesn't matter whether you are running for the state legislature or president of the United States. Brilliant organization, unlimited resources, and the effective use of technology all in the hands of bright people who are driven by the more than just simple ideology create the most formidable campaign strategy imaginable."

—Tom Tancredo,
former US representative (R-CO)

"Let's assume Pat Stryker and Tim Gill disappeared tomorrow, the whole infrastructure is still there. The concept to get communities of interest together is still there. Are the Republicans ever going to pull in the same direction? Common sense says no."

—Bill Menezes,
former head of Colorado Media Matters

"Either we can sit around and whine about the fact that a couple hyper-rich, supersmart people have been throwing us around like the political equivalent of a rag doll, or we can dust ourselves off, raise the level of our game, and get back in the fight. That means first modernizing those time-tested, traditional messages so that our voice breaks through the noise and the smear and the distortions—it's the message of Reagan. It's a message that affirms the goodness of this country, the greatness of the American Dream. I mean, since when did rugged individualism become uncool? When did high taxes and a nanny state that micromanages your life come back into fashion? The answer is, they didn't. Republicans have become wimps—we don't make the case with courage or conviction. And we just have to. I always ask young people if they like [New York] Governor [David] Patterson's plan to tax iPod downloads. Here's the summary of their opinion: absolutely not, no way, not ever. At which point the wisdom of Reagan settles in on that young person. So the message matters most and we've got to sharpen it."

—Josh Penry,
Colorado state Senate minority leader (R)

Index

About the Authors

Adam Schrager covers politics for KUSA-TV, the NBC affiliate in Denver, Colorado. In twenty years in the business, he has won numerous broadcast journalism accolades, including more than fifteen Emmy Awards. He has a bachelor's degree in history from the University of Michigan and a master's degree in journalism from Northwestern University. Schrager's first book, *The Principled Politician: Governor Ralph Carr and the Fight against Japanese American Internment*, has been praised by historians and politicians nationwide. The biography, which chronicles former Colorado governor Ralph Carr's defense of Japanese Americans after Pearl Harbor, led state lawmakers to name the state justice center and a Colorado state highway after Carr. Schrager, his wife, and their two children live in the Denver area.

Rob Witwer is a former member of the Colorado House of Representatives. He has successfully managed several local campaigns and has served as legal counsel to the Colorado Republican Party, the governor of Colorado, and several legislative, congressional, and gubernatorial candidates. He has a bachelor's degree in political science from Amherst College and a law degree from the University of Chicago Law School. Witwer practices law in Denver and lives in Golden with his wife and four sons.